Hiking the Lake Placid 9

Help Us Keep This Guide Up to Date

Every effort has been made by the author and editors to make this guide as accurate and useful as possible. However, many things can change after a guide is published—trails are rerouted, regulations change, facilities come under new management, and so forth.

We appreciate hearing from you concerning your experiences with this guide and how you feel it could be improved and kept up to date. While we may not be able to respond to all comments and suggestions, we'll take them to heart, and we'll also make certain to share them with the author. Please send your comments and suggestions to the following address:

FalconGuides
Reader Response/Editorial Department
64 South Main Street
Essex, CT 06426

Thanks for your input, and happy trails!

Hiking the Lake Placid 9

A Guide to the Adirondack Hiking Challenge

James Appleton

FALCON GUIDES

ESSEX, CONNECTICUT

FALCONGUIDES®

An imprint of The Globe Pequot Publishing Group, Inc.
64 South Main Street
Essex, CT 06426
www.globepequot.com

Photos by James Appleton unless otherwise noted
Maps by The Globe Pequot Publishing Group, Inc.

British Library Cataloguing-in-Publication Information Available

Library of Congress Cataloging-in-Publication Data
Names: Appleton, James, 1986– author
Title: Hiking the Lake Placid 9 : a guide to the Adirondack hiking challenge / James Appleton.
Description: Essex, Connecticut : FalconGuides, [2026] | Summary: "A guidebook to completing the Adirondacks' Lake Placid 9 hiking challenge successfully, equipping hikers with the practical knowledge they need to plan, train, and hike each peak efficiently and safely"— Provided by publisher.
Identifiers: LCCN 2025052227 (print) | LCCN 2025052228 (ebook) | ISBN 9781493096008 paperback | ISBN 9781493096015 epub
Subjects: LCSH: Hiking—New York (State)—Lake Placid | Hiking—New York (State)—Adirondack Mountains | Hiking—Equipment and supplies | Lake Placid (N.Y.) | Adirondack Mountains (N.Y.) | BISAC: SPORTS & RECREATION / Hiking | LCGFT: Guidebooks
Classification: LCC GV199.42.N652 A67 2026 (print) | LCC GV199.42.N652 (ebook)
LC record available at https://lccn.loc.gov/2025052227
LC ebook record available at https://lccn.loc.gov/2025052228

A bluebird Adirondack summer day on Mount Van Hoevenberg.

This guidebook is dedicated to my wife, Kinnon. Thank you for helping me create and run the Lake Placid 9'er hiking challenge from the ground up, for building the LP9 website, for stuffing endless finisher envelopes, and for going on this adventure of life with me. I am a blessed man to have you.

This book is also dedicated to my little LP9 helpers and daughters, June, Penny, and soon Rosemary. Thanks for stickering the envelopes and handing me the patches when I'm filling the envelopes. We make a great team!

Midday summer hike up Van Hoevenberg with my wife, Kinnon.

Contents

Overview

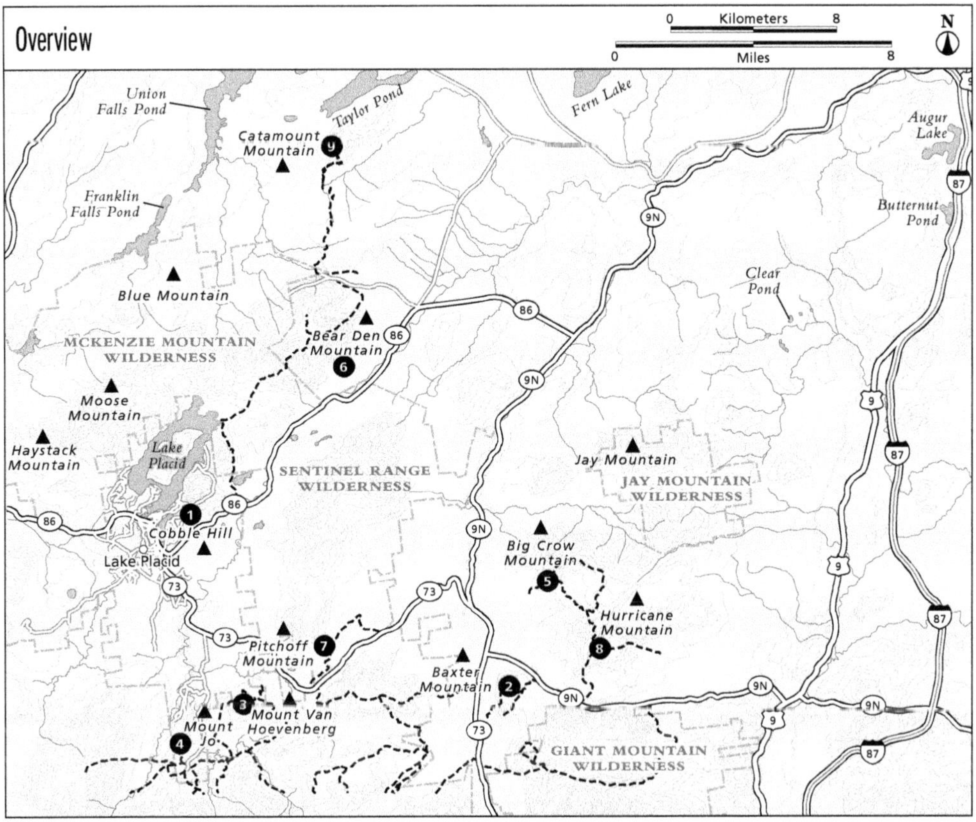
0 Kilometers 8
0 Miles 8
N
Union Falls Pond
Taylor Pond
Fern Lake
Augur Lake
Catamount Mountain
9
Franklin Falls Pond
Butternut Pond
87
9N
Clear Pond
Blue Mountain
86
Bear Den Mountain
6
MCKENZIE MOUNTAIN WILDERNESS
Moose Mountain
Haystack Mountain
Lake Placid
SENTINEL RANGE WILDERNESS
Jay Mountain
JAY MOUNTAIN WILDERNESS
1
Cobble Hill
Lake Placid
Big Crow Mountain
5
73
Hurricane Mountain
Pitchoff Mountain
7
8
Baxter Mountain
2
3
Mount Van Hoevenberg
Mount Jo
4
GIANT MOUNTAIN WILDERNESS

Preface

Hiking these mountains changed my life, and they can do the same for you.

If you're looking for mountain adventures that will get the whole family outdoors, ignite your soul, and give you unbelievable summit views—you've found it. The nine mountains of the Lake Placid 9'er each have a story to tell. They'll teach you about nature, about life, and about yourself. Mountains have a unique way of revealing both our shortcomings and our strengths. They help us clear our minds. They show us where we need to improve in our lives. They also showcase strengths we often didn't even know we had—the mountains are funny that way.

With every step on every trail, you're writing your own adventure story, and the mountains are the backdrop. Every peak is a different character with its own unique chapter in that story. It's my hope that you'll discover the story these nine mountains are telling you and the lessons they're teaching you, and tell that adventure story for the rest of your life. The mountains have a way of transforming us. And what a privilege it is to climb them.

This guidebook will give you the information you need to have a safe, successful, and fulfilling mountain adventure here in the Adirondack Park. There's way more to the Adirondacks than just the 46 High Peaks, and the LP9 will show you that.

It's time to go and write your LP9 story. Let's begin the journey.

Acknowledgments

These nine mountains changed the trajectory of my life personally and professionally. Writing a guidebook about them has been a true honor.

Thank you to Mason Gadd, Meredith Dias, Rhonda Baker, Amanda Wilson, and rest of the team at FalconGuides for believing in this project and helping bring it to life with professionalism and care.

To the Lake Placid 9'er crew—aka my wife and daughters—thank you for the countless hours supporting hikers, stuffing and filling finisher envelopes with me, and keeping this challenge running strong. A special shout-out to the Lake Placid Post Office staff who patiently handstamp every single envelope so finishers get their patches. You are part of this story too.

Thank you to the thousands of Lake Placid 9'er finishers who have climbed these peaks, shared your stories with me, and sent kind notes about this list of mountains.

Thank you to the landowners around Cobble Hill and Baxter Mountain for allowing the hiking public to access these special places, and to the organizations across the Adirondack Park who work tirelessly to protect and preserve this Forever Wild landscape.

To my family, friends, and podcast listeners—thank you for the endless support of all my endeavors.

Thank you to Lake Placid and the Adirondack Mountains—it is a true privilege to call this place home, to explore your trails, and to stand on your summits.

And finally, thank you for reading this guidebook. These nine mountains are going to give you an Adirondack adventure you will never forget. See you on the trails!

Meet Your Guide

James Appleton is an Adirondack native and the creator of the Lake Placid 9'er challenge. He lives in Lake Placid, New York, with his wife and three daughters. He's the host of the premier podcast, *The 46 of 46 Podcast*, where he brings the Adirondacks' mountains, trails, lakes, and stories to life. Since launching in 2019, the podcast has been downloaded over half a million times worldwide. He has been praised in reviews as a "natural born storyteller" and "the voice of the Adirondacks."

Hiking mountains, however, wasn't always part of James's life. Far from it, in fact. Despite growing up in Lake Placid surrounded by mountains, he always hated hiking. Why? Because hiking mountains is hard. From turning around on mountains, to bonking, to feeling like death on every summit, most of his hiking experiences ended poorly. It wasn't until after a physical fitness transformation and losing over 70 pounds in his late twenties that James suddenly found himself in a new phase of life. A stronger, lighter, fitter phase.

One spring day in 2018, on a whim, he decided to give hiking another try. Ampersand Mountain was on tap that day in his quest to finish the Saranac Lake 6'er challenge once and for all. It had been five years since he last went hiking thanks to a rough outing on McKenzie Mountain, where he swore off hiking forever. But things change.

The hike up Ampersand that day was different though. For the first time in his life, he flew up the mountain with ease. No burning legs. No heart beating

James enjoying a perfect fall day on Mount Jo. JORDAN CRAIG

out of his chest gasping for air. Instead, he hiked from the trailhead to the summit without stopping—a new experience entirely compared to every other hike of his life. A new level of adventure was unlocked that day, and it changed the trajectory of his life forever.

Fast forward to today, and James is a multi-round Adirondack 46'er and has written three other books about hiking and the Adirondacks—including a guidebook on the 46 High Peaks. James is a licensed hiking guide and professional strength coach who has worked with over 300 hikers worldwide, helping them build the same strength and endurance for climbing mountains that he built. The exact strength and endurance that allowed him to finally live the adventurous life he always dreamed of. His passion lies in helping others unlock their own ability to enjoy hiking mountains instead of suffering through them. He's experienced both sides of that coin firsthand, which makes his coaching so powerful.

The mountains transformed James's life inside and out, and his goal is to help anyone who wants to experience that same transformation. Whether it's through his podcasts, books, fitness coaching programs, or the Lake Placid 9'er challenge, James's mission is simple and consistent: to help people have strong, safe, successful, and *fulfilling* mountain adventures.

Other books from James include *The Adirondack 46 in 18 Hikes: The Complete Guide to Hiking the High Peaks*; *Hike Strong: The Complete Guide to Building Strength, Endurance, and Confidence for Hiking and Backpacking*; and *Adirondack Campfire Stories: Tales and Folklore from Inside the Blue Line.*

Introduction

About the Lake Placid 9

Thirty-plus miles of trail. Ten thousand-plus feet of elevation gain. Nine mountains. One unforgettable Adirondack hiking adventure.

Nestled in the heart of New York's Adirondack High Peaks, the Lake Placid 9'er is a hiking challenge made up of nine sub-4,000-foot mountains around the greater Lake Placid region. Each peak offers an unparalleled hiking experience for new and seasoned hikers alike.

While the 46 High Peaks serve as the main Adirondack hiking attraction, the Lake Placid 9 all offer High Peaks–caliber views for a fraction of the effort. Each mountain is unique—with elevations ranging from 2,300 feet to roughly 3,700

Summer on Mount Jo. JONATHAN ZAHAREK

feet—and can be hiked in half a day or less, making these mountains perfect for the family, new hikers, an afternoon hike, or to warm up your trail legs.

The Lake Placid 9 is a great introduction to hiking in the Adirondacks, and serves as the ultimate stepping-stone to confidently climb the 46 High Peaks. If you're new to hiking or new to the Adirondacks, these mountains are the best place to start.

List of the Lake Placid 9 by Elevation (feet):

1. Cobble Hill—2,343 feet
2. Baxter Mountain—2,440 feet
3. Bear Den Mountain—2,650 feet
4. Big Crow Mountain—2,815 feet
5. Mount Jo—2,876 feet
6. Mount Van Hoevenberg—2,940 feet
7. Catamount Mountain—3,169 feet
8. Pitchoff Mountain—3,497 feet
9. Hurricane Mountain—3,678 feet

Adirondack Hiking Challenges

Hiking challenges are part of the culture in the Adirondacks. A "hiking challenge" is simply a peak-bagging list. Hikers summit each mountain on the designated list, and

The new staircase on the Mount Jo Long Trail.
JONATHAN ZAHAREK

then upon completion they can send in a registration form and get a finisher's patch. It's the Adirondack brand. Some hiking cultures and towns are all about backpacking trails; however, in the Adirondacks it's all about climbing mountains. Steep elevation gains, tough trails, beautiful summits, and patches. That's the Adirondack way.

Challenges big and small exist all over this 6-million-acre outdoors paradise, and they all offer a unique adventure. From the mighty Adirondack 46 High Peaks to the Lake Placid 9, Saranac Lake 6, Firetowers Challenge, Lake George 12, Tupper Lake Triad, and more, there's no shortage of lists to hike and mountain adventures to be had.

The LP9 has emerged as the premier "low peak" hiking challenge in the Adirondacks. The iconic nature and history of Lake Placid creates part of the draw. The other part of the draw is the location. The LP9 sits in and around the 46 High Peaks, giving hikers High Peaks views from each of these beloved "smaller" mountains.

These peak-bagging challenges are terrific because they give people goals to work toward and a curated adventure. They often bring people to new places and new mountains they wouldn't have known about otherwise, thus spreading out the foot traffic around the Adirondack Park. Plus, who doesn't love getting a patch for their efforts and having a tangible representation of their hiking memories? I certainly do.

Once hikers complete the Lake Placid 9, they can submit their hike information and registration form at www.LakePlacid9er.com to receive their official LP9 finisher's patch and sticker.

The LP9 Origin Story

The Lake Placid 9'er challenge was created to solve a problem and fill a need.

Most hikers and Lake Placid locals only know about the High Peaks. Therefore, most people will automatically default to hiking a High Peak simply because they are unaware of anything else. From my experience I have found most Lake Placid locals can only name three mountains: Mount Marcy (the tallest peak), Cascade Mountain (the most popular peak), and Mount Jo (a local favorite). This causes people to unknowingly get in over their head in the mountains, ultimately resulting in a suffer fest they weren't physically, mentally, or logistically prepared for or, worse, a search and rescue. The region's smaller mountains, or "low peaks" needed the spotlight shined on them.

The other problem I saw was that there wasn't a curated list of mountains that progressed in a linear fashion serving as a good "warm-up" to hiking the High Peaks. A list of mountains that could take a new hiker from the couch to High Peaks–ready by the end. A list where each mountain built on the last, getting progressively taller and harder. Like a linear progression training program in the gym, I wanted to build a linear progression mountain list.

So I created it.

The mountains were chosen in a strategic manner with two primary goals in mind:

- Showcase the Lake Placid region's amazing smaller mountains.
- Create a list that could help new hikers go from novice to High Peaks–ready over the course of the challenge.

Enter the Lake Placid 9'er. A carefully crafted list of mountains that fulfills both of those goals.

There were other parameters I stuck to for this list as well, such as:

- Each mountain had to be in Lake Placid, or roughly one town over.
- Each mountain had to be a half-day hike or less.
- Each mountain needed clear summit views worth visiting many times over.

After some hard work hiking all of the peaks again just to be sure, building a website with my wife, buying patches and stickers, promoting it online, finding some local sponsors—and doing it all simply for the love of the game and the desire to fill a need—the Lake Placid 9'er was officially born.

What started from an idea in the summer of 2018 is alive and well today, with new finishers completing the challenge every week. To date there are over 3,000 Lake Placid 9'er finishers, from new hikers to world-class adventurers, in every season. We've had over one hundred ultra finishers who completed all nine in 24 hours. We've had finishers as young as 5 and as young as 85. And most importantly, the LP9 has helped kick-start the "hiking careers" of hundreds and hundreds of hikers from around the country (I know because they tell me on their registration form). It's done what it was designed to do, and more.

As you read this guidebook, I hope you're excited to go on a journey through the Adirondack mountains unlike any other. Each of these nine mountains has its own story to tell and adventure to offer you.

Let's start planning your adventure!

Planning Your LP9 Adventure

How to Hike the Lake Placid 9

The LP9 was put together to serve as a stepping-stone to the 46 High Peaks; therefore, if you have Adirondack 46'er aspirations, these smaller mountains will help you build the experience and confidence to tackle that adventure. If you're an experienced hiker you can choose to hike the nine peaks in whatever order you see fit. However, if you're new to hiking in the Adirondacks, or to hiking in general, I recommend climbing them in the order listed here. That way each hike builds on the last in various levels of difficulty ranging from mileage to elevation gain, time, and

Fun clouds from Mount Van Hoevenberg.

terrain. While there's no wrong route, and the order can certainly vary slightly, I've found this to be the best route through the LP9 when starting out.

Hiking the LP9 in Order of Difficulty for New Hikers

1. Cobble Hill—2,343 feet
2. Baxter Mountain—2,440 feet
3. Mount Van Hoevenberg—2,940 feet
4. Mount Jo—2,876 feet
5. Big Crow Mountain—2,815 feet
6. Bear Den Mountain—2,650 feet
7. Pitchoff Mountain—3,497 feet
8. Hurricane Mountain—3,678 feet
9. Catamount Mountain—3,169 feet

Hiking Multiple Peaks in One Day

The Lake Placid 9 is made up of nine individual peaks, each with its own trailhead parking. This means that you can't link mountains together; rather each peak will involve ascending and descending the mountain in its entirety before heading to the next trailhead.

Many of these mountains can be hiked together in a single day, however, since they're all a half-day or less hike. Some advanced hikers have even summited all nine in a single 24-hour day. As of the writing of this book, the current Fastest Known Times (FKT) for completing the LP9—including total drive time between peaks—is a lightning fast 7 hours, 34 minutes, 4 seconds by Nick Arndt in 2020, and on the women's side, 9 hours, 36 minutes, 24 seconds by Bethany Adams in 2025. While most people can't compare themselves to these elite-level mountain athletes, it does highlight that hikers can certainly climb multiple peaks in a single day.

The mountains can be grouped together by both level of difficulty and geographic location. Here is how to pair the mountains together to hike multiple peaks in a single day based on these two factors.

Grouped via Level of Difficulty

1. Big Crow and Baxter Mountain
2. Cobble Hill, Mount Jo, Mount Van Hoevenberg
3. Bear Den and Catamount
4. Pitchoff Mountain
5. Hurricane Mountain

Grouped via Geographical Location

1. Big Crow, Baxter Mountain, Hurricane Mountain (Keene, NY, area)
2. Cobble Hill, Mount Jo, Mount Van Hoevenberg, Pitchoff Mountain (Lake Placid, NY, area)
3. Bear Den and Catamount (Wilmington, NY, area)

The Long Weekend LP9'er

The Lake Placid 9'er is often completed in one long but jam-packed weekend of hiking. The mountains and trailheads are grouped in clusters. If your goal is to complete them all in a weekend, I recommend hiking them based on their geographic locations. Here's an itinerary you can follow; however, feel free to switch days around how you see fit.

Day 1: Hurricane, Big Crow, Baxter

Day 2: Pitchoff, Mount Jo, Mount Van Hoevenberg, Cobble Hill

Day 3: Bear Den, Catamount

Now that you know how to break up the nine mountains, let's dive into where to go to hike these mountains—let's talk trailheads.

Cobble Hill with my daughter June, age 4.

Trailheads

Each mountain has its own designated trailhead. Some mountains, however, have multiple trailhead and route options.

Cobble Hill

GPS coordinates (trailhead): 44.29333°N, 73.97139°W

The trailhead is in Lake Placid, at the corner of the Northwood School entrance and Mirror Lake Drive. You will see a trailhead sign and a wooden bridge to begin the hike. From the intersection of Route 73 and Route 86 in Lake Placid, follow Route 86 toward the center of town. Take a right at the town hall onto Mirror Lake Drive. Continue through the four-way stop and follow Mirror Lake Drive past Northwood Road to the entrance to Northwood School. Park just up the street along Mirror Lake Drive or on Main Street and walk around Mirror Lake to the trailhead.

Mount Jo

GPS coordinates (trailhead): 44.1825°N, 73.96639°W

From Lake Placid, go east on Route 73 past the Olympic Jumping Complex to Adirondack Loj Road. The trailhead parking lots are 5 miles from Route 73 at the Adirondack Loj. Note that there is a parking fee for the Loj and this trailhead fills up fast on summer/fall weekends. From the parking lot at the High Peaks Information Center at the end of Adirondack Loj Road, return to the entrance station and find the trail at the far corner of the snowplow turnaround. Head toward Heart Lake and walk along the lake until you arrive at the Mount Jo trail junction on the right (with the lake to your left).

Baxter Mountain

GPS coordinates (trailhead): 44.2205°N, 73.7492°W

Leave Lake Placid on Route 73 and head west, toward Keene. Continue through Keene and turn left on Route 9N toward Elizabethtown. Continue for about 2 miles to the top of the hill and park at the trailhead on the right—look for the Department of Environmental Conservation (DEC) sign. If you come to a tavern, you have gone a bit too far.

Mount Van Hoevenberg

Van Hoevenberg East Trailhead at Mount Van Hoevenberg Olympic Sports Complex: The Van Hoevenberg Olympic Sports Complex is located at 31 Van Hoevenberg Way in Lake Placid off Route 73 between Lake Placid and Keene. Look for trailhead signs between the bobsled track and the main building at the facility.

GPS coordinates (trailhead): 44.1937°N, 73.9548°W (South Meadows)

South Meadows Trailhead: From the intersection of Route 86 and Route 73 in Lake Placid, follow Route 73 toward Keene. Continue for 4 miles to Adirondack Loj Road on the right. Follow this road for another 4 miles to Meadow Lane on the left. Follow Meadow Lane for 0.25 mile to the trailhead on the left.

Big Crow Mountain

GPS coordinates (trailhead): 44.2609°N, 73.7330°W

Crow's Clearing Trailhead: From Lake Placid, go 15 miles east on Route 73 to Keene. At 200 yards past the intersection with Route 9N in Keene, turn left on Hurricane Road at the Keene Town Hall. At just over 2 miles from Route 73, bear left onto the dirt road called O'Toole Lane and continue for 1.2 miles to the end at Crow's Clearing. The trail to Big Crow begins on the left side of the clearing. Note that the latter portion of this road is unplowed during winter. Hikers will have an additional 0.3-mile walk up the road to the trailhead. Park at your own risk along the road.

Bear Den Mountain (at Whiteface Mountain)

GPS coordinates (trailhead): 44.3595°N, 73.8576°W

Whiteface Mountain Ski Resort, Bear Den parking lot: From the intersection of Route 73 and Route 86 in Lake Placid, follow Route 86 toward Wilmington. Continue for 9.2 miles to the Whiteface Mountain Ski Center. Turn into the ski center and follow the road around to the right to the Bear Den parking lot. You'll see the trailhead signs. Note that sometimes the gate on the road is closed; hikers will have to park in an outer lot at Whiteface Mountain Ski Resort and walk down the road to the trailhead.

Pitchoff Mountain

GPS coordinates (trailhead): 44.21917°N, 73.88694°W

From the intersection of Route 73 and Route 86 in Lake Placid, follow Route 73 toward Keene. Continue on Route 73 for 7.5 miles to the Pitchoff West Trail. For Pitchoff East Trail, continue 2.7 miles farther on Route 73. Both trailheads are on the left, but parking is along the right shoulder for the East trailhead. Be careful when crossing this busy road.

Catamount Mountain

GPS coordinates (trailhead): 44.4431°N, 73.8799°W

From the four-corner intersection in the village of Wilmington, head west up Route 431. At the intersection with the Whiteface Memorial Highway, just before the toll house, bear right toward Franklin Falls (CR 72 or Gillespie Drive on some maps). Continue for 3.3 miles to Roseman Road and take a right. Follow Roseman Road for 0.8 mile and turn right on Plank Road. Follow that for 2.2 miles, to the parking area on the left. Note there is no cell phone service at this trailhead.

Hurricane Mountain

GPS coordinates (trailhead): 44.21139°N, 73.72306°W (Route 9N Trailhead/Southern Approach)

Take Route 73 east from Lake Placid and turn left onto Route 9N after 15.5 miles. The parking area is 3.5 miles up the road on both sides. The trailhead is on the left.

Baxter trailhead sign on Route 9N.

GPS coordinates (trailhead): 44.2609°N, 73.7330°W (Crow's Clearing Trailhead)

Crow's Clearing Trailhead: From Lake Placid, go 15 miles east on Route 73 to Keene. At 200 yards past the intersection with Route 9N in Keene, turn left on Hurricane Road at the Keene Town Hall. At just over 2 miles from Route 73, bear left onto the dirt road called O'Toole Lane and continue for 1.2 miles to the end at Crow's Clearing. The trail to Big Crow begins on the left side of the clearing. Note that the latter portion of this road is unplowed during winter. Hikers will have an additional 0.3 mile walk up the road to the trailhead.

Permits and Parking

No permits are necessary for any of the Lake Placid 9 mountains or trailheads. Parking is always on a first-come, first-served basis. Please obey traffic laws and only park in designated parking spots.

The only trailhead with a parking fee is Mount Jo, where parking is at the Adirondack Loj. Once arriving on the Adirondack Mountain Club property, a parking pass can be purchased at the small booth at the entrance to the parking lots. As of the writing of this guidebook, the parking fee is $15. The Adirondack Mountain Club trailhead is also one of the primary trailheads for many of the Adirondack 46 High Peaks, so be aware this trailhead can fill up fast on the weekends in the summer.

Weather and Seasons

The Lake Placid 9 mountains can be hiked year-round and serve as a fantastic option during shoulder seasons (winter/spring and fall/winter), when the higher-elevation mountains are covered in new or old snow and mud. In the spring these mountains dry out much faster and become the go-to mountains to hike as we all prepare for summer hiking. The fall foliage views are spectacular from every mountain on the list, with Mount Van Hoevenberg taking the top seed. Van Hoevenberg's summit is my personal favorite viewpoint in the Adirondack Park for fall foliage due to its view of South Meadow and the High Peaks above. You will want to visit this summit during peak foliage season, trust me.

The LP9 mountains also serve as a great option for beginner winter hikers as well. Just like I recommended earlier for those new to hiking, the same applies to anyone new to winter hiking. If you hike all nine in the order of difficulty listed earlier, each mountain will build on the last and you can gain experience, dial in your winter hiking gear and layers, and learn the unique demands of winter hiking on smaller peaks first. In fact, that's exactly what I did when I first began winter hiking before heading up the High Peaks. Winter hiking is quite different from summer/fall hiking, and while the risk is significantly higher, I'd argue the reward is much higher too. You will never forget the first time you summit a mountain in the dead of winter and see the landscape covered in white, fluffy, Dr. Seuss–style snow. It's truly magical.

Camping and the LP9

While there are many places to camp around the Adirondacks, from state campgrounds to tent sites and lean-tos deep in the backcountry, the Lake Placid 9 mountains do not have many places to camp on the trail. These mountains are all typically hiked in half a day or less, thus not requiring camping.

With that said, the Gulf Brook Lean-to is a great option to camp during your Lake Placid 9'er journey if you're looking for a quiet overnight in the woods. Starting at Crow's Clearing Trailhead (Big Crow and Hurricane Northern Approach), the lean-to sits on the Gulf Brook Trail along with a few tent campsites, at the junction with the Northern Approach trail up Hurricane Mountain. You could camp here while hiking Hurricane Mountain and Big Crow Mountain for a fun weekend. As a bonus hike, I recommend hiking the Soda Range loop ending on Big Crow before coming back to your campsite.

Adirondack lean-to.

Campfires

Outside of a pure survival situation, there will be no need to build a campfire during your Lake Placid 9'er journey. Per NYS regulations, fires are only permitted in designated campfire pits at designated campsites.

Almost Time to Hit the Trail

Now that you have a rundown of what the Lake Placid 9'er challenge is, what mountains you'll hike, where the trailheads are, let's talk about preparing for the adventure. The more prepared you are, the higher the chances of success, and the more likely you are to have a fulfilling, enjoyable Adirondack Mountain adventure.

Let's dive into gear, pre-hike homework, hiking etiquette, and more so that you and everyone else can have an enjoyable hiking experience.

Views from the Pitchoff East trail.

Cobble Hill with my wife, Kinnon.

Before You Hit the Trail

Trail Tips and Hiking Etiquette

Like anything, hiking is an activity with plenty of unwritten rules meant to be followed for the good of the land, the trails, the experience, the wildlife, and fellow hikers. Etiquette goes a long way in life and on the trail. Here are some tips to remember before you hit the trail.

Trail Tip: Hiking Pace
Everyone's got their own rhythm out here, and that's okay. If your hiking partner moves faster, let them go ahead and plan to meet at a trail junction or viewpoint periodically. Just don't split up if the trail is confusing—stick together and take it slow. The mountain isn't going anywhere, and slow and steady usually wins.

Trail Tip: Kids on the Trail
Hiking with kids is an adventure all its own. Start small, see how they do, and expect plenty of snack breaks (and maybe a piggyback ride back to the car). The primary goal with kids isn't the summit, it's making the day fun so they'll want to come back.

Trail Tip: Sounds of the Park
One of the best parts of the Adirondack Park is the sounds of the Adirondack Park: the wind, a rushing stream, birds singing, chipmunks running through the leaves. So tuck the phone away, leave the speakers at home, and keep your voices down.

Trail Tip: Stick to the Plan
If you're hiking with others, don't wander off without telling them. Disappearing in the mountains isn't fun for anyone.

Trail Tip: Stay on the Trail
Mud? Walk straight through it. Switchbacks? Take every one of them. Trails are built the way they are for a reason. When you step off to rest, do it on rock or hard ground so you're not trampling plants. If you're above tree line, rock-hop your way across and avoid stepping on the precious and rare alpine vegetation.

Trail Tip: Share the Trail
When people catch up to you, step aside and let them pass. And when you're coming downhill, remember that uphill hikers have the right of way. It's good trail manners. A smile and a "how's it going?" never hurt either. In fact, it's weirder to pretend the other person doesn't exist. Be friendly.

Trail Tip: If You Carried It In, Carry It Out
If it fits in your backpack on the way up, it fits in your backpack on the way down. Every wrapper, every peel. Even the apple core that you think is "natural." Leave the mountain looking like you were never there.

Trail Tip: Respect the Wildlife
The woods aren't our home; we're just visitors. Watch animals from a distance, don't chase them for photos, and definitely don't feed them. A squirrel doesn't need your granola bar, and a bear learning about people-food is bad news for everyone.

Leave No Trace

The Leave No Trace Center for Outdoor Ethics (www.lnt.org) is a Colorado-based organization whose mission is to teach people how to enjoy the outdoors while minimizing their impact on the land, water, wildlife, and trails. After all, it's important for us to treat the outdoors with respect and remember that we are guests in the wilderness.

The 7 Principles of Leave No Trace are worth learning and applying in all your outdoor pursuits:

1. **Plan ahead and prepare:** Study the map, know your route, make a game plan for your hike, and have everything you need for a safe and successful day in the backcountry.
2. **Travel and camp on durable surfaces:** Stay on the trails, avoid walking on fragile vegetation ("do the rock walk"), and camp in designated campsites.
3. **Dispose of waste properly:** Take all trash out with you including apple cores and banana peels. When going "number 2," dig a 6-inch cat hole in the ground, 200 feet off the trail and 200 feet away from water sources. After you take care of your business, fill in the hole and cover with leaves.
4. **Leave what you find:** Don't pick that pretty flower you're eyeballing, take a photo instead. Leave it for the next person to enjoy just like you did.
5. **Minimize campfire impacts:** Only make campfires in designated preexisting campfire rings (where permitted). Fires are prohibited in the eastern and central zones of the High Peaks Wilderness (see official zoning on the High Peaks map).
6. **Respect wildlife:** View animals from afar with your eyes and keep your voices low. Remember, you're a guest in their home.
7. **Be considerate of other visitors:** Be respectful and don't take away from other people's outdoor experience, the same way you don't want them to take away from yours.

Navigation Resources: Map, Compass, and GPS

Map and Compass

Wherever you're hiking it's important to have the area's official map in your backpack. Study the map before every hike to learn your route, bail-out points, and notable landmarks. The night before new hikes I often find myself going through the map all night long in my head: *Ok, I go right at the first trail junction, then a mile later take a left at the second junction just after the river crossing, followed by an immediate right that will take me to the summit.*

uncertainty and offer reassurance that you're on the correct trail. Peace of mind in the woods is worth its weight in gold.

Pre-Hike Homework

Whether you're heading 8 miles deep into the backcountry or hiking a mountain a half mile from the road, it's your responsibility to always do your pre-hike homework. It's important to remember that the mountains don't care about you, and even on a short hike, things can go wrong. The more prepared and knowledgeable you are about your hike, the better the odds are for success. Here is the pre-hike homework I go through before every hike, whether hiking the Lake Placid 9, the 46 High Peaks, or anywhere else in the world.

Learn Your Route

- Map: Study your map beforehand and learn what key features to look for, where your trail junctions are, along with elevation gains.
- Water sources: Identify where water sources are to refill your water if needed (be sure to bring a water filtering/purification method). It's always better to carry more water than you expect to need.

Check the Weather

- Check the weather for the week leading up to your hike, not just the day you're planning to hike. High rainfall that week means high rivers, heavy snowfall might mean breaking trail, etc.
- Use sites like mountain-forecast.com to get the most accurate picture of weather conditions at various elevations.
- Pay special attention to weather changes like thunderstorms, snow, or extreme heat/cold—especially on higher peaks where weather conditions can shift quickly.

Bail-Out Points

- It's crucial to know your bail-out points where you can safely turn around if you need to or call an audible if you need to cut your hike short due to weather, fatigue, time, injury, etc.

Share Your Plan

- Let someone know where you're going, what trails and mountain(s) you're hiking, and how long you expect to be out there.

Physical Readiness for Hiking Mountains

When it comes to hiking, I'm a firm believer that your physical fitness is more important than your gear. It doesn't matter what fancy equipment is in your backpack if your legs and lungs can't take you to the summit and back. It's important to always assess your physical readiness and choose a hike that meets you where you're at. Hiking mountains can be a tough experience when climbing peaks that are above your current skill level.

If you're unsure about your fitness level, I recommend hiking the LP9 in the order of difficulty listed earlier. This way you start on the smaller hikes and build up mountain by mountain. Remember that this list of mountains was put together specifically to help people go from the couch to the summit. If your fitness level isn't High Peaks–ready, the LP9 will help you get there. Follow the plan by hiking the mountains in the recommended order and watch your abilities and fitness level for hiking mountains improve with each peak.

Later in the book I'll offer more perspective and insight on how to improve your physical ability for hiking mountains so you arrive at every trailhead feeling strong and confident, and don't have to worry about suffering through hikes. More on that later though.

Next let's talk about being properly prepared with the right gear.

Equipment and Gear

Being prepared for the mountains is critical for success and having an enjoyable experience. Let's go through what to have in your backpack to ensure you're prepared with the right gear to have a successful mountain adventure.

The 10 Essentials

The 10 Essentials is a list of essentials that the outdoors community collectively agrees should be in every hiker's backpack when they head into the backcountry. While some of these items may be overkill on smaller mountains like some of the Lake Placid 9, it's always better to be overprepared than under. Anything can happen out there, so prepare accordingly. The 10 Essentials are:

1. Navigation (map, compass, GPS)
2. Sun protection (hat, sunscreen, sunglasses)
3. Insulation (extra clothing for warmth, even in summer)
4. Illumination (headlamp, extra batteries)
5. First-aid kit (Band-Aids, tourniquet, ace bandage, etc.—know how and when to use what you bring)
6. Fire-making supplies (lighter, matches, firestarter)
7. Repair kit (knife, multi-tool, duct tape, hockey tape)
8. Nutrition (enough food for the hike, plus extra)
9. Hydration (water and purification system)
10. Emergency shelter (bivy, tarp, or space blanket)

James enjoying the iconic view on Mount Jo. JORDAN CRAIG

James's honorable mentions include:

11. Rain jacket—even on bluebird, sunny days. Weather can change quickly.
12. Zip ties—these fix packs, zippers, tents, snowshoes, and so much more in a pinch.
13. Paracord—comes in handy when you get caught out there and are forced to spend the night unexpectedly.

Winter add-ons include:

- Snowshoes (required when snowpack is 8 inches or more)
- Microspikes (September through May)
- Insulated winter hiking boots
- Hat, gloves, face protection
- Base layer (thermals), mid-layer (fleece), top layer (wind/water protection coat)
- Sunglasses/ski goggles
- Full change of clothes (*no* cotton clothing)
- Space blanket or bivy sack

Now that we've covered what should be in your backpack, let's move on to what should be on your body.

Clothing

First things first, you'll want to avoid cotton clothing whenever possible because it doesn't wick moisture away from your body and doesn't dry if it gets wet. Wet clothes can lead to problems and even hypothermia on the trail during any season, so it's important to wear moisture-wicking materials that keep you warm and can be easily adjusted. Dress for the elements and remember that it may be warm at the trailhead, but the summit could be a wildly different experience. Anticipate the summit temperature being 10 to 20 degrees cooler than the trailhead.

A layering system for cool weather and winter hiking should include:

1. Base layer: a moisture-wicking layer (merino wool or synthetic)
2. Mid-layer: a fleece or lightweight coat for hiking, and a puffy insulated jacket for warmth when stopped
3. Top layer: a shell to repel wind and water

Note: It's a good rule of thumb to always bring a jacket for warmth on the summit, even in the summer months. I recommend at least bringing a light fleece just in case.

Footwear

The proper footwear can make or break your hike from a physical, mental, and logistical perspective. Whether you're hiking in boots or trail runners, it's paramount that your footwear is designed for the elements and terrain you're hiking in. Hiking mountains is no place for the wrong shoes. Take this seriously, especially here on the Lake Placid 9. I recommend shoes that are broken in, feel comfortable for long miles, have good tread, and are at minimum water resistant.

Additional Gear

Trekking Poles

While trekking poles are not a necessity by any means to go hiking, I believe they're worth their weight in gold. Trekking poles help spread out the workload that your body is undergoing, which helps your legs go farther with less fatigue. With poles your back and arms do a lot of the work every time you step up on the ascents, and they help take pressure off your knees on the descents. Consider adding trekking poles to your hiking gear list, and you'll quickly see why most hikers use them in the mountains.

Traction: Microspikes and Snowshoes

Microspikes are a must-have in your backpack while hiking the LP9 mountains for the majority of the year. I recommend having them in your pack for the taller peaks from October to May. During the shoulder season months, it may seem like spring or fall at the trailhead, but the conditions could be much different on the summit. It's a safe choice to carry microspikes for this reason outside of the late spring/summer/early fall months. Ice can make the trail dangerous to climb without the proper traction on your feet. With the proper traction, it becomes business as usual.

Hiking mountains in the winter will require microspikes and snowshoes all season long, so please plan accordingly. Note the difference between microspikes and crampons. Microspikes will be sufficient for the LP9 in most conditions.

A subzero winter day inside the Hurricane fire tower.

Food and Water

Food is your body's fuel. When you're hiking in the mountains, your body is working hard and therefore will need that fuel to get you to the summit and back to the trailhead. It's best to have more "fuel" than you think you'll need, because it's better to have it and not need it than need it and not have it.

I recommend having 1 to 2 liters of water per mountain and plenty of high-quality food that includes protein, carbs, and fats. Light snacks throughout your hike, especially during the ascent, will help keep your body energized. Aim for 75 to 100 calories per hour as a good rule of thumb.

Trail Nutrition 101

Here's a quick lesson on nutrition and how it impacts your body so you know what food to reach for to be successful when hiking. Just eating random food is suboptimal. The best approach is eating the right food at the right time so your body performs at its best.

Protein—for staying full and overall performance. It's hard to perform and hike well if you're hungry. Think meat, beef jerky, protein bars, etc. Reach for high-protein food every few hours to keep your stomach satisfied so your body can perform better. Eat a high-protein meal before and after hikes as well. Your body will need the protein to recover after the hike.

Carbohydrates—for quick energy bursts right now. Carbs are your body's primary energy source, which it will constantly burn; therefore, you'll want to continuously "top off your tank" throughout your hikes for good energy. Think energy gels, honey, sugary snacks, fruit, and bread. Reach for simple carbs when you're feeling low on gas and need a shot of energy.

Fats—for sustained energy throughout the day. Think of fats as your energy reserve tank. Fats are higher in calories and take longer to burn, so they are a good source of sustained energy throughout the day. Think trail mix and nut butters. Reach for fats periodically throughout the day to keep calories coming in to ensure your fuel tank remains full. Note that fats take longer to digest and will not give you the quick burst of energy you may be seeking like carbohydrates do.

The Ultimate Hiking Meal: The Summit Sandwich

A tasty, hearty sandwich with meat, cheese, bread, and veggies is the perfect choice for day hikes like the Lake Placid 9 because it checks all the nutrition boxes (protein, carbs, and fats). It will give you the proper fuel your body needs to hike well. Protein from the meat and cheese, carbs from the bread, and fats from the cheese and condiments create the perfect energy source. A well-crafted peanut butter and jelly sandwich is another good option as well.

A sandwich offers real substance, which will help your body perform better on the trail. Plus, it's the perfect item to enjoy while gazing at the majestic summit views.

The ultimate summit snack—the summit sandwich.

Pre-Hike Checklist

- ☐ Did you study your map and memorize the route?
- ☐ Did you check the weather in the mountains for the days prior to the hike?
- ☐ Do you have more food and water than you anticipate needing?
- ☐ Do you have the right gear in your pack (layers, raincoat, essentials, etc.)?
- ☐ Are your shoes/boots comfortable and suitable for the terrain?
- ☐ Did you tell someone your plan, route, and when you expect to return?

It looks like you're ready to hit the trail. Let's next talk about the nine mountains that make up the Lake Placid 9'er.

Map Legend

Boundaries

- National forest/park
- National monument/ wilderness/wildlife refuge
- State/county/preserve /wilderness

Transportation

- Freeway/Interstate Highway
- US Highway
- State Highway
- County/Forest Road/Other
- Railroad
- Featured Route
- Trail or Fire Road

Hydrology

- Medium River
- Small Pond/Lake
- Small River/Creek
- Marsh/Swamp
- Waterfall

Symbols

- Trailhead
- Picnic Area
- Visitor/Information Center
- Parking
- Restroom
- Campground
- Mountain/Peak
- Building/Point of Interest
- Scenic View/Viewpoint
- Tower
- Inn/Lodging
- Town

The Hikes

In this chapter we'll get to know the nine peaks of the Lake Placid 9'er so you can be confident and prepared for your hikes. Here I list the mountains in the order I recommend hiking them if you're a new hiker. When hiking the LP9 in this order, each peak will build in difficulty on the last. This way hikers can build up their ability and confidence with every mountain. If you're a seasoned hiker, feel free to climb them in whatever order you desire.

Enjoy your journey through the Lake Placid 9'er. It's going to be one to remember!

Hiking the LP9 in Order of Difficulty for New Hikers:

1. Cobble Hill—2,343 feet
2. Baxter Mountain—2,440 feet
3. Mount Van Hoevenberg—2,940 feet
4. Mount Jo—2,876 feet
5. Big Crow Mountain—2,815 feet
6. Bear Den Mountain—2,650 feet
7. Pitchoff Mountain—3,497 feet
8. Hurricane Mountain—3,678 feet
9. Catamount Mountain—3,169 feet

1 Cobble Hill (2,343 feet)

Cobble Hill sits above Mirror Lake overlooking the village of Lake Placid. This mountain may be modest in elevation, but it's massive in heart. It's one of the most obtainable big views in the Adirondacks. Cobble Hill is one of those quintessential "short trail, big payoff" type of peaks. For decades it's been a favorite for locals, families, first-time hikers, and anyone wanting a quick escape into the woods without the grind of the High Peaks.

At just 0.8 mile to the summit, this short climb gives you a front-row seat to the remote Sentinel Range, the High Peaks, and the Lake Placid village below. It's also one of the most accessible mountains in the Adirondacks, sitting just steps from downtown Main Street Lake Placid on Mirror Lake Drive. It offers a truly unique Adirondack experience—one minute you're on Main Street Lake Placid, then minutes later you're on a mountain deep in the woods.

When strolling down Main Street Lake Placid, Cobble Hill is easy to spot across Mirror Lake thanks to the bald cobble on its face, hence the name. It's the perfect hike for anyone kicking off their Lake Placid 9'er journey.

Start: Northwood School and Mirror Lake Drive
Elevation gain: 465 feet
Summit elevation: 2,343 feet
Distance: 1.6 miles out and back
Difficulty: 2 out of 7, moderate
Hiking time: 1–3 hours
Seasons: All seasons
Fees/permits: None
Pets: All dogs must be on leash.
Trail surface: Rocky
Land status: Private and public (Saranac Lakes Wild Forest)
Nearest town: Lake Placid, NY
Water availability: None
Amenities available: None
Sunrise or sunset: Sunrise
Views: Outstanding views of Sentinel Range, High Peaks, and Lake Placid

FINDING THE TRAILHEAD: The trailhead is in Lake Placid, at the corner of the Northwood School entrance and Mirror Lake Drive. You will see a trailhead sign and a wooden bridge to begin the hike. From the intersection of Route 73 and Route 86 in Lake Placid, follow Route 86 toward the center of town. Take a right at the town hall onto Mirror Lake Drive. Continue through the four-way stop and follow Mirror Lake Drive past Northwood Road to the entrance to Northwood School. Park just up the street along Mirror Lake Drive or on Main Street, and walk around Mirror Lake to the trailhead. **Trailhead GPS:** 44.29333°N, 73.97139°W

The Hike

The brand-new trailhead (as of 2024) is located at the corner of Mirror Lake Drive and Northwood School's driveway. From here, a 250-foot wooden boardwalk leads you into the woods before the trail turns to well-groomed dirt. The first section is

Cobble Hill with my daughter June, age 7.

gentle, winding left and right before beginning a steady climb. About a half mile in, you'll come to a junction. Stay straight to continue toward the summit. This is when the elevation gain begins.

The trail has a few short periods of climbing that will get your heart rate elevated. The upper section is steeper, as the trail runs up and along the rock slab (this slab is visible from Main Street), offering unparalleled views of Main Street Lake Placid below, so make sure you turn around and enjoy the view.

After climbing up the slab, at around 0.7 mile, you'll continue past the old trail junction to Echo Pond. From here turn right, and just steps later you'll be on Cobble Hill's first rocky summit ledge. For such a small mountain, the view is a big surprise: the village of Lake Placid spread out below, the Olympic Jumping Complex, the Sentinel Range in the forefront, and the High Peaks filling the horizon. It's especially beautiful at sunset, though make sure you pack a headlamp for the walk down. For the best view, continue over the summit to the other side and head back into the woods on the trail. A minute or two later you'll come out onto the true summit where the big views await.

For the descent, return the way you came. Much of this trail is on private land, so be extra respectful.

Cobble Hill

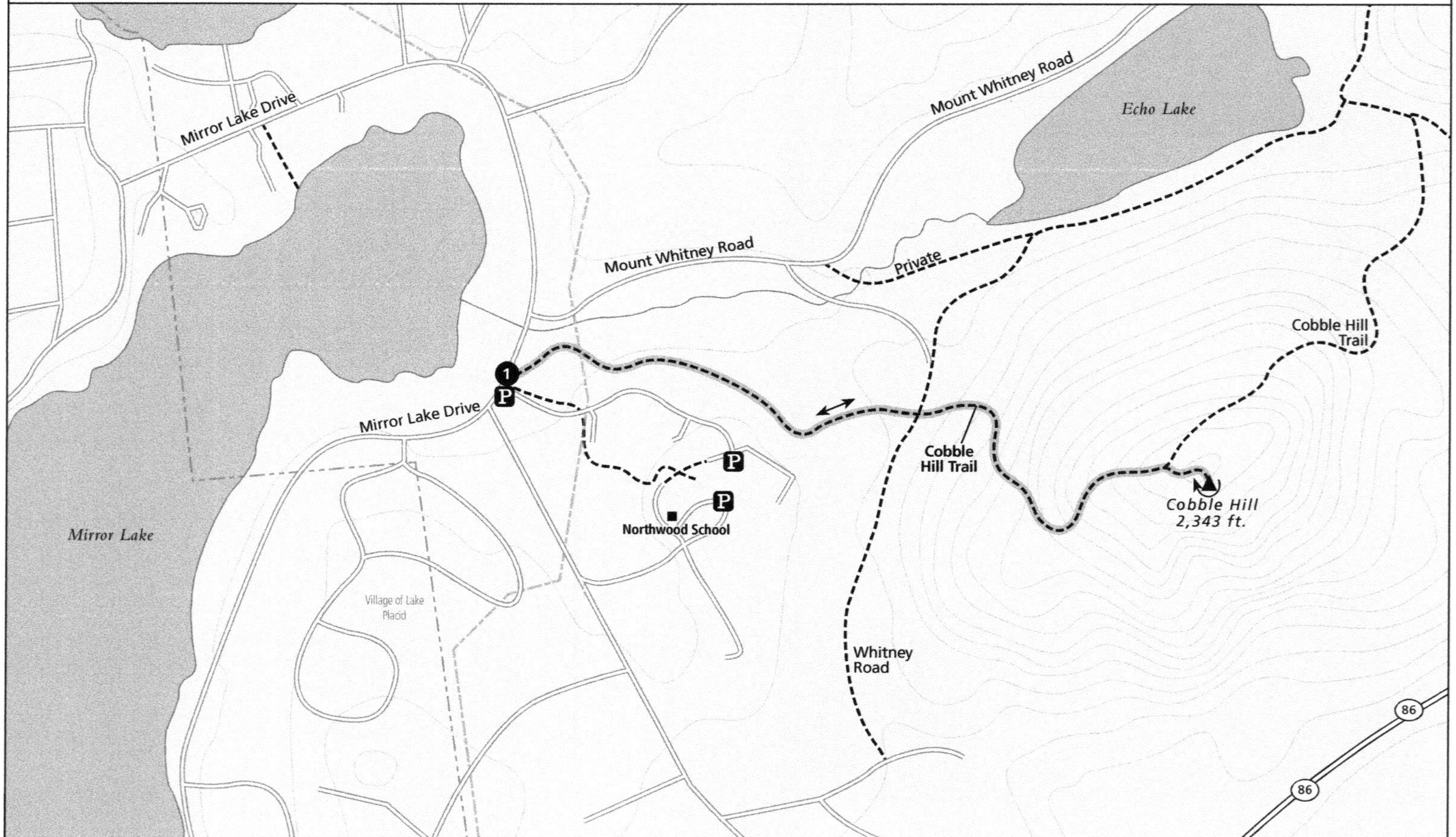

0
Kilometer
0.5
0
Mile
0.5
N
Mirror Lake Drive
Mount Whitney Road
Echo Lake
Mount Whitney Road
Private
Cobble Hill
Trail
1
P
Mirror Lake Drive
P
P
Northwood School
Cobble
Hill Trail
Cobble Hill
2,343 ft.
Mirror Lake
Village of Lake
Placid
Whitney
Road
86
86

Miles and Directions

0.0 Start at the trailhead on the side of Mirror Lake Drive and the entrance of Northwood School. Begin on the 250-foot wooden boardwalk.

0.4 The trail crosses an old road and starts gaining elevation.

0.5 Climb the rock slab or the trail just to the side of the slab. Follow the trail markers as you go.

0.7 Arrive at the first summit lookout. Continue over the summit and back into the woods toward the true summit.

0.8 Reach the true summit. Descend the same trail to return to the trailhead.

1.6 Arrive back at the trailhead.

Other Routes

At one time there was a trail that went along Echo Pond, making this a loop hike, but that trail is now closed as of the writing of this guidebook.

Background, History, and Fun Facts

Cobble Hill is a hometown hike for Lake Placid locals and has been for a long time thanks to trails across private land that allow hikers access to this gem of a mountain. It was always popular because of its proximity to town and its viewpoint, but until recently, parts were rough, muddy, slick, and sometimes confusing.

In 2023–2024 Northwood School (on whose land much of the trail crosses) joined with community partners such as the Adirondack Land Trust, Town of North Elba, DEC, Lake Placid 9'er, and others to reimagine the trail. A new trailhead was built at the corner of Mirror Lake Drive and Northwood School's driveway along with an updated route up the mountain. From a 250-foot boardwalk over marshland, to new bridges, reroutes, and improved drainage, the trail is now safer and more sustainable than ever.

Despite its small size, Cobble Hill is a Lake Placid staple. It's also a prime example of how organizations, private landowners, and citizens can come together with a common goal of creating sustainable access and preserving the land we all love for the good of the Adirondacks. Community stewardship continues to make this modest "hill" shine.

2 Baxter Mountain (2,440 feet)

Baxter Mountain is the definition of a family favorite. At just 1.4 miles to the top, this short, gradual hike delivers some of the best views you'll find without committing to a full High Peaks hike. Located in the Hammond Pond Wild Forest between Keene and Elizabethtown, the trail starts right off Route 9N, just up the hill from the intersection with Route 73 and across the street from Hurricane Road. It's the kind of hike locals often sneak in after work, bring the kids on for a first summit, or add on to a day of other hiking. It's the type of mountain that is worth many visits.

Start: Baxter Mountain NY 9N Trailhead
Elevation gain: 741 feet
Summit elevation: 2,440 feet
Distance: 2.8 miles out and back
Difficulty: 2 out of 7, moderate
Hiking time: 1.5–3 hours
Seasons: All seasons
Fees/permits: None
Pets: All dogs must be on leash.
Trail surface: Smooth and rocky
Land status: Private and public (Hammond Pond Wild Forest)
Nearest town: Keene, NY
Water availability: None
Amenities available: None
Sunrise or sunset: Sunset
Views: Sentinel Range and Giant Mountain views

Finding the Trailhead: Leave Lake Placid on Route 73 and head west, toward Keene. Continue through Keene and turn left on Route 9N toward Elizabethtown. Continue for about 2 miles to the top of the hill and park at the trailhead on the right—look for the DEC sign. If you come to a tavern, you have gone a bit too far. **Trailhead GPS:** 44.2205°N, 73.7492°W

The Hike

The trail begins gently, marked with blue NYSDEC markers, and eases you into the hike with a gentle start through the woods. Almost immediately you'll pass through a power-line cut before climbing gradually through a mixed forest of white birch, hemlock, and fir trees. At about 0.2 mile you'll step up some broad log stairs, and by 0.4 mile the trail bends sharply to the right and begins working its way uphill in a series of switchbacks. The elevation gain is never too punishing, and the trail is relatively clear of rocks and roots, which is perfect for younger hikers or those new to the Adirondacks.

As you climb, the forest begins to change. Near the 1.0-mile mark you'll start encountering open ledges. At 1.0 mile, a small lookout on your left offers a clear view of the fan-favorite High Peak, Giant Mountain, rising above the nearby hills. It's important to note the first mile of this trail is on private land, and the landowners have graciously allowed the public to access this wonderful trail, so be extra respectful. Here you'll pass a state wild forest boundary sign, and the trail begins to open up more frequently onto rocky slabs. Now the real fun begins!

Late fall on Baxter.

The stretch from 1.0 to 1.3 miles is where Baxter truly shines. A series of open ledges appear one after another. This stretch sometimes gets confusing, but the trail will reveal itself as you climb up these small ledges. Once getting up them the first views await you, and they're worth enjoying. Hikers often sit and take in these views before and after getting to the true summit. It's the perfect place to enjoy a snack or

The beloved trees on top of Baxter.

Trail signs on Baxter Mountain.

Baxter Mountain

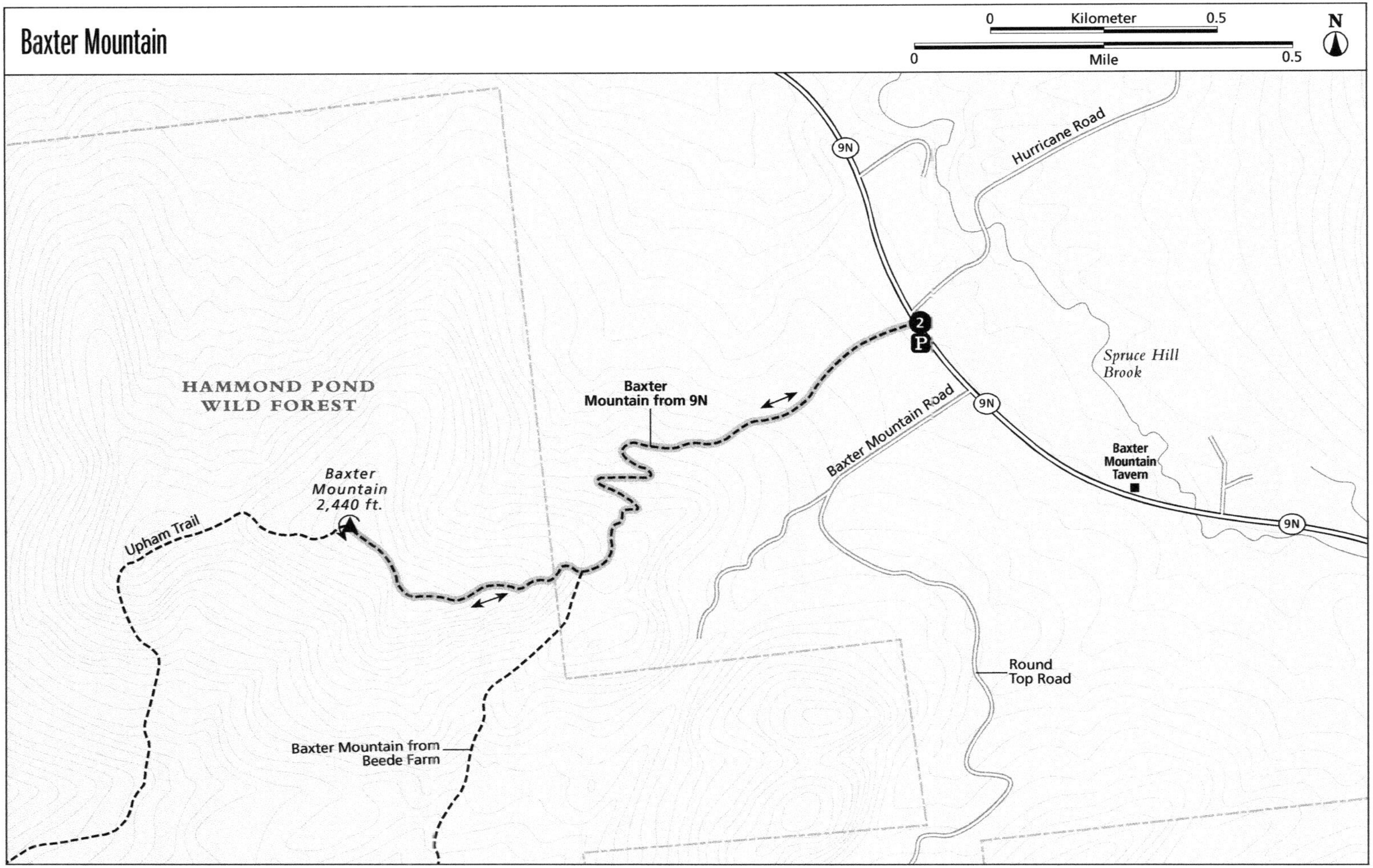

a well-earned summit sandwich. From these ledges you'll see the iconic and memorable Baxter Mountain pine trees—you'll know them when you see them—along with views of Giant Mountain dominating the foreground, the Great Range to the southwest, and fellow Lake Placid 9'er Hurricane Mountain standing tall to the east with its fire tower viewable on top.

The official summit, however, is still up the trail. So after enjoying the first view, continue up the trail. At about 1.4 miles, after another light slab climb, the true summit is just off the trail, marked by a small boulder with a cairn in the trees. But there are many open rock ledges here in various directions, all offering grand views of peaks across the valleys, including Nippletop and other High Peaks. This mountain truly is one of the best "low peaks" in the Adirondacks.

Return to the trailhead the same way you came, retracing your steps down the switchbacks and through the birch and fir forest. Round-trip, the hike comes in just under 3.0 miles and makes for an easy half-day adventure with views that rival mountains twice its size.

Miles and Directions

0.0 Start at the trailhead on the side of NY 9N.

0.1 Walk through power lines.

0.2 Climb the log staircases.

0.5 Hike through the switchbacks, then continue the main trail.

0.9 Trail junction with Beede Trail. Go right toward the summit.

1.0 First viewpoint.

1.2 Approaching another viewpoint.

1.3 Hill ascends a little steeper, continuing on the trail and not the ledge.

1.4 Arrive at the true summit. It's recommended to return the way you came.

2.8 Arrive back at the trailhead.

Other Routes

There are other trails up Baxter such as the Beede Trail starting from Beede Farm Road, which meets the Baxter 9N trail a mile in, and the Upham Trail, which goes up the back side of the peak. All of these trails begin on private land, so be respectful. I recommend hiking from the primary Route 9N Trailhead.

Background, History, and Fun Facts

Baxter Mountain may not be the tallest peak of the Lake Placid 9, but it has quietly become one of the most beloved. Sitting between Elizabethtown and Keene, it rises gently above the valley, offering a short climb with summit views that keep locals coming back regularly.

The name "Baxter" is believed to come from an early resident of Keene Flats, often cited as Benjamin Baxter in local lore. The mountain shows up as early as 1876 on maps of Essex County. Through the late nineteenth and early twentieth centuries, Baxter became a vantage point for photographers and painters who wanted to capture Keene Valley and the surrounding ranges. Historic photos in the Keene Valley Library archives show how often people climbed this mountain just to record the view. Some things never change, right?

More recently, Baxter has taken on new conservation significance. In 2024, one family donated 107 acres on the mountain's southern slopes and along the East Branch of the Ausable River to the Adirondack Land Trust, who then transferred it to the New York State Forest Preserve. That gift not only protects valuable floodplains and forest, but also ensures that Baxter's ridgeline views, which are visible from Route 73 and Marcy Field, will stay forever wild.

The trail itself has evolved over the years as well. Old, steep paths gave way to new routes with switchbacks to make it more accessible to families and newer hikers. Sometimes there's confusion over which spot counts as the "true summit" because the first lookout often gets mistaken for it—but that's part of Baxter's charm. When you think you're at the summit, just keep going—you're almost there. Regardless of whether you stop at the first set of ledges or continue on to the cairn marking the actual top, the views are some of the best for the effort in the Adirondacks.

Baxter may be small compared to the High Peaks, but that's what makes it special. It's a mountain that keeps you coming back for more. And it doesn't take all day to explore it.

3 Mount Van Hoevenberg (2,940 feet)

Completed in 2018, the Van Hoevenberg East Trail is one of the newest and most well-built trails that the Adirondack Park has to offer. The East Trail showcases the gold standard in trail sustainability, and it shows with every step. The summit offers some of the best views you will find anywhere in the Adirondacks. In fact, it is my number one favorite view in the Adirondacks for fall foliage. You'll want to plan to enjoy this summit view for a while.

Start: Mount Van Hoevenberg Olympic Sports Complex
Elevation gain: 885 feet
Summit elevation: 2,940 feet
Distance: 3.8 miles out and back (East Trail) / 4.0 miles point to point (South Meadows)
Difficulty: 2 out of 7, moderate
Hiking time: 1.5–3 hours
Seasons: All seasons
Fees/permits: None
Pets: All dogs must be on leash.
Trail surface: Smooth and rocky
Land status: Private and public (High Peaks Wilderness and Saranac Lakes Wild Forest)
Nearest town: Lake Placid, NY
Water availability: None
Amenities available: Mount Van Hoevenberg Olympic Sports Complex
Sunrise or sunset: Sunrise
Views: A top-5 view in the Adirondack Park

Finding the Trailhead: Van Hoevenberg East Trailhead at Mount Van Hoevenberg Olympic Sports Complex: The Van Hoevenberg Olympic Sports Complex is located at 31 Van Hoevenberg Way in Lake Placid off Route 73 between Lake Placid and Keene. Look for trailhead signs between the bobsled track and the main building at the facility.

The Hike

Once arriving at the Mount Van Hoevenberg Olympic Sports Complex, begin walking toward the main building. You will see hiking trail signs between the bobsled track and the main building. Follow the trail up along the wall of the bobsled track to the official trailhead register.

The trail immediately begins gaining elevation in a light, but consistent manner, filled with many steps as it goes along the facility's mountain coaster ride. After 0.3 mile the trail levels off as it runs along the eastern flanks. About a mile into the hike, the trail switchbacks to the right and continues to climb. There are many staircases throughout, from the trailhead to the summit. This hike is a family-friendly hike due to its gentle elevation gain and terrain.

Once arriving on the summit, you'll pass a lookout on the left, while the main summit ledge is a few more feet up the trail where my favorite view in the Adirondack Park awaits. Get ready to say, "*Wow!*"

The South Meadows trail comes out on the other side of the summit ledge.

Summer perfection on Mount Van Hoevenberg staring at the High Peaks.

Mount Van Hoevenberg (East)

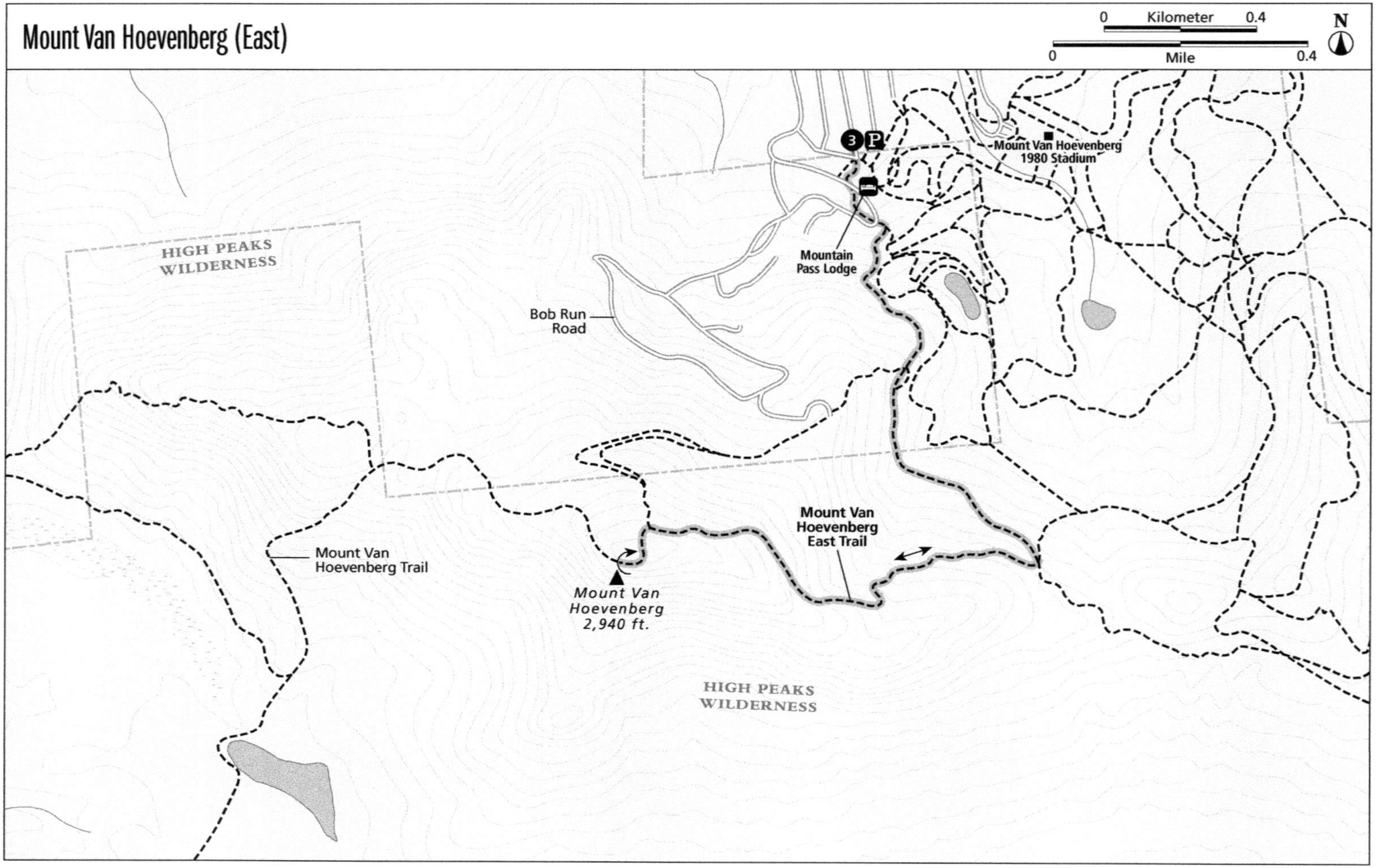

Miles and Directions

East Trail

0.0 Start at the trailhead, located by the Mountain Pass Lodge and bobsled tracks.

0.5 Arrive at the intersection for the Mount Van Hoevenberg loop. It is recommended to stay straight toward the summit.

0.9 Continue straight on the trail, following the switchback to the right.

1.7 Reach the intersection for the Mount Van Hoevenberg loop. Keep going straight toward the summit.

1.9 Arrive at the true summit ledge. You can return the way you came or choose to traverse and go down the Van Hoevenberg Trail to South Meadows (this will require two vehicles, one parked at each trailhead).

3.8 Arrive back at the trailhead.

A winter sunset on Van Hoevenberg.

Other Routes

The other route up Van Hoevenberg starts at the South Meadows Trailhead. From the intersection of Route 86 and Route 73 in Lake Placid, follow Route 73 toward Keene. Continue for 4 miles to Adirondack Loj Road on the right. Follow this road for another 4 miles to Meadow Lane on the left. Follow Meadow Lane for 0.25 mile to the trailhead on the left. **Trailhead GPS:** 44.1937°N, 73.9548°W

The trail begins with a 1.0-mile straight, flat walk through a beautiful old pine forest before coming out to a beaver pond. From here the summit ledge is visible, and the trail wraps around to the left of the pond before beginning to climb. This trail is reminiscent of a typical Adirondack hiking trail, whereas the newer East Trail showcases current sustainable trail building. The trail climbs the western side of the mountain and enjoys multiple light, yet consistent climbs to the summit. This trail gains 826 feet of elevation over 1.1 miles of climbing once leaving the pond. This is similar to what hikers will find in some places in the Adirondack High Peaks.

Miles and Directions

Mount Van Hoevenberg (South Meadows) Trail

0.0 Start at the trailhead on South Meadows Road, on the left.

0.8 Arrive at the beaver pond. Walk to the left around the pond.

1.0 Begin climbing along a steady grade

2.1 Arrive at the summit. You can choose to keep going toward the Olympic Sports Complex or return the way you came.

4.2 Arrive back at the trailhead on South Meadows Road.

Background, History, and Fun Facts

Mount Van Hoevenberg may only stand at 2,940 feet, but few mountains on planet Earth carry a story as unique as this one. This mountain blends the Adirondack backcountry with an Olympic legacy, along with a summit view that rivals the best in the park.

The mountain was named for Henry Van Hoevenberg, the visionary behind the original Adirondack Loj, just a couple of miles away. But while Henry left his mark as a pioneer of outdoor recreation in the Adirondacks, this mountain became famous for something different: bobsledding.

In 1930, as Lake Placid prepared to host the 1932 Winter Olympics, Mount Van Hoevenberg was chosen to house North America's first permanent bobsled track. Engineers carved a 1.5-mile-long track into its slope, made up of twenty-six turns sending athletes down the mountainside at lightning speeds. It was the start of a sliding sports legacy that continues to this day. By the time the 1980 Winter Games rolled around, Van Hoevenberg had grown into one of the premier sliding sports venues in the world.

Mount Van Hoevenberg (South)

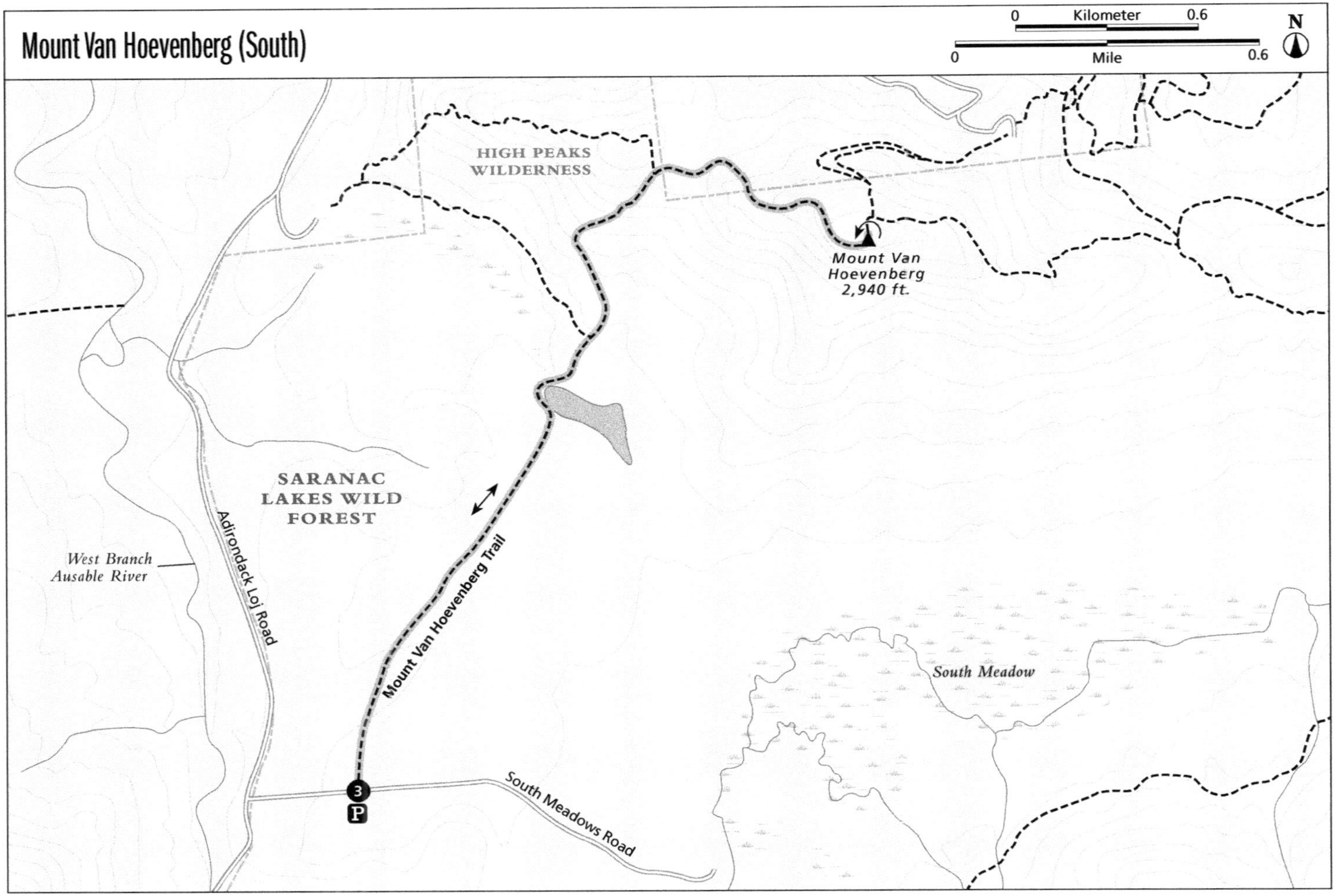

Fall foliage on Mount Van Hoevenberg. My favorite view in the ADK for foliage.

Today, the modernized track welcomes Olympians and World Cup bobsled, luge, and skeleton athletes every year and is heavily used for world competitions at the highest level. So when you're hiking Van Hoevenberg, check out this storied bobsled track because it's one of only sixteen on the planet.

Outside of its Olympic legacy, Mount Van Hoevenberg is far more than just a sliding sports complex. Its summit reveals one of the most breathtaking views in the Adirondacks. Ask ten Adirondack hikers where their favorite fall foliage view is, and you'll probably get ten different answers. If you ask me, I'll tell you without hesitation: Van Hoevenberg is number one.

What makes this mountain so special is the way it brings everything together, from its Olympic history to its trails and summit view. From Olympic athletes chasing medals to families chasing foliage and adventure, pound for pound Mount Van Hoevenberg holds one of the most unique stories in the Adirondacks—and arguably the world.

4 Mount Jo (2,876 feet)

Mount Jo is one of the most popular hikes in Lake Placid for good reason—High Peaks–caliber views for minimal effort. In fact, the summit view from Mount Jo is arguably the most iconic view in the Adirondacks (along with the famous Indian Head lookout). This mountain offers two trails up/down or can be hiked as a loop trail, which I recommend. The Long Trail is a more gradual climb and better for new hikers, while the Short Trail is a much steeper climb, like what you'll experience in the High Peaks. The two trails rejoin prior to the summit.

Start: Adirondack Loj
Elevation gain: 700 feet
Summit elevation: 2,876 feet
Distance: 2.6-mile loop
Difficulty: 4 out of 7, moderate
Hiking time: 1–3 hours
Seasons: All seasons
Fees/permits: $15+ parking fee at Adirondack Loj
Pets: All dogs must be on leash.
Trail surface: Rocky
Land status: Adirondack Mountain Club
Nearest town: Lake Placid, NY
Water availability: None
Amenities available: The Adirondack Loj, High Peaks Information Center, Hungry Hiker
Sunrise or sunset: Both
Views: One of the most iconic views of the High Peaks

Finding the Trailhead: From Lake Placid, go east on Route 73 to Adirondack Loj Road, which is the first right after the ski jumps. The trailhead parking lots are 5 miles from Route 73 at the Adirondack Loj. Note that there is a parking fee for the Loj and this trailhead fills up fast on summer/fall weekends. From the parking lot at the High Peaks Information Center at the end of Adirondack Loj Road, return to the entrance station and find the trail at the far corner of the snowplow turnaround. **Trailhead GPS:** 44.1825°N, 73.96639°W

The Hike

If you're looking for one of the best bang-for-your-buck hikes in the Adirondacks, Mount Jo is it. It's a local favorite for good reason. At just over a mile to the summit, this short but rewarding climb gives you an open ledge summit with one of the most iconic views of the Adirondack High Peaks. It's the perfect option for families, new hikers, or anyone who wants a half-day hiking adventure with a big Adirondack payoff.

The trail starts at the Adirondack Loj parking lot and eases you in with a flat stroll to the shores of Heart Lake. You'll walk past a small cabin along the way that is occasionally open with nature exhibits. After following the lake for a short stretch, look for the signs pointing you toward Mount Jo. The Mount Jo trail junction is on the right (with the lake to your left). Before you start up, however, go enjoy the lookout view on Heart Lake directly across from the Mount Jo trail junction. The mountain

The MacIntyre Range and Mount Colden from Mount Jo.

towering above the lake in front of you is the Adirondack High Peak known as Wright Peak (4,580 feet).

About a quarter mile later you'll reach a junction where the trail splits into two options: the Short Trail to the right, and the Long Trail straight ahead. Both trails get you to the top, but they feel very different. The Short Trail is, true to its name,

Trail signs at the Adirondack Loj. JONATHAN ZAHAREK

shorter—just 0.2 mile less round-trip—but it's also steeper, more rugged, and more like what you'll experience in the High Peaks. The Short Trail will test your conditioning more than the long one. The Long Trail is more gradual and much friendlier for groups or families. A lot of hikers like to go up one way and down the other. If you're unsure, take the Long Trail up.

From the trail junction, the climb begins on the Short Trail, where you'll tackle rocky steps—boulders left over from the last ice age—as you work your way north toward the summit. The trail has markers from 1 to 10 throughout this hike, breaking it up in sections. Sections 4 to 7 are the bulk of the climb. Stone steps help keep your feet dry as small streams crisscross the path. Near the top you'll climb a series of fun but steep wooden staircases that lead you onto open rock slabs. From there, the summit is just through the trees.

At about 1.2 miles from the trailhead, you'll step out onto Mount Jo's summit ledges—a rocky knob facing Heart Lake as the mighty MacIntyre Range towers above front and center. The MacIntyre Range is Algonquin, Wright, and Iroquois; Mounts Colden and Marcy sit in the distance along with many other High Peaks. To your right you'll see Street and Nye and even Santanoni. There are multiple viewpoints around the summit, so take your time and soak it all in. It's hard to believe this magnificent and iconic Adirondack view comes with such a short hike.

For the descent, you can return the way you came or follow the Long Trail down. Be careful going down the staircase near the summit since it's steep. The Long Trail is smoother, with dirt paths, gentler grades, and fewer rocks. Along the

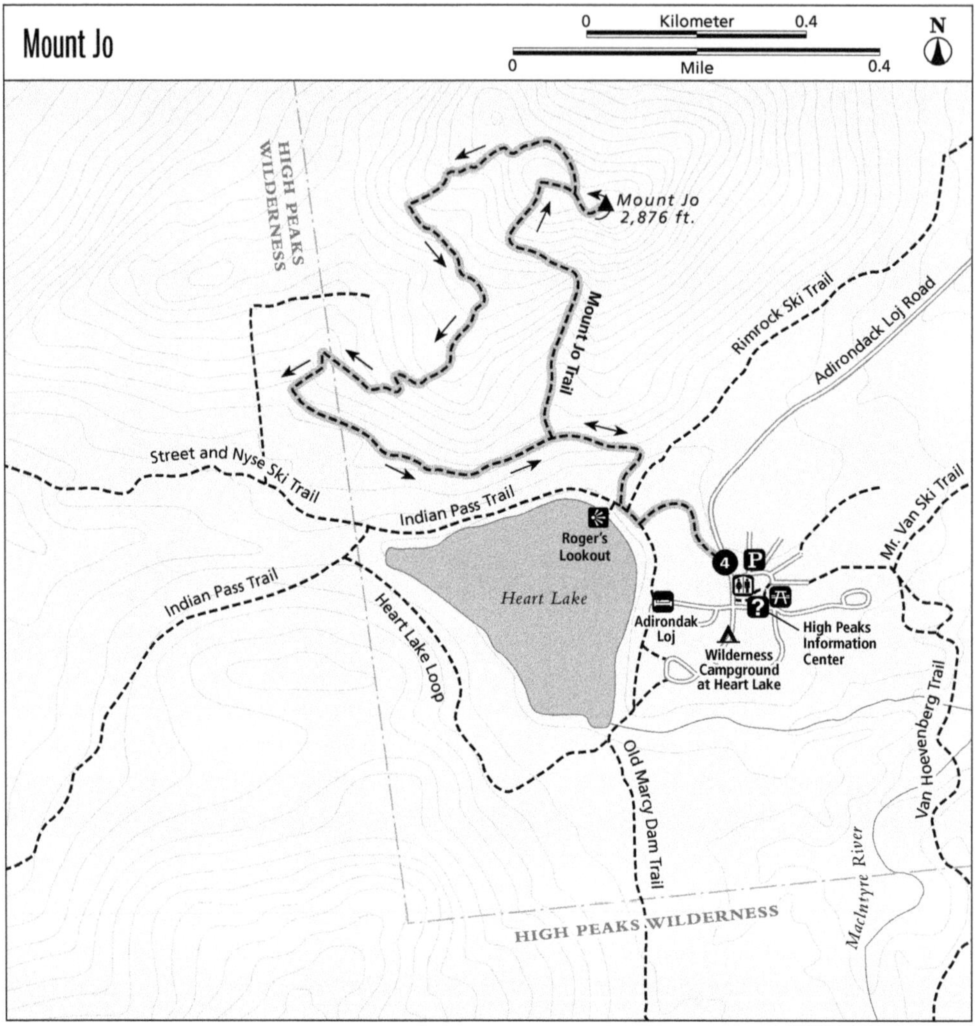

way you'll pass a 25-foot rock wall and some wooden staircases before rejoining the Short Trail at 2.1 miles. From there it's a straightforward walk back down to the trail register and Heart Lake before turning left to go back to the Loj, finishing at about 2.6 miles round-trip.

Miles and Directions

0.0 Start at the trailhead, located at Adirondack Loj.

0.2 Arrive at the Mount Jo trail loop. Keep following the trail toward the intersection for the Mount Jo Long and Short Trails.

0.5 Trail junction for the Mount Jo Long Trail (left) and Short Trail (right); go right.

1.0 Arrive at the intersection with the Long Trail.

The view from Mount Jo. Painting by Andrew Silbert.

1.1 Climb the three-ladder staircases.

1.2 Arrive at the summit.

1.4 Arrive back at the intersection with the Long Trail.

1.6 Meet the intersection with the Rock Garden Trail; continue on the Long Trail.

2.1 Finish the Long Trail; arrive back at the loop intersection.

2.6 Arrive back at the Adirondack Loj parking lot.

Other Routes

The Short Trail and Long Trail are the only trails up Mount Jo and can be hiked as a loop (as described here) or an out and back on either trail. The Short Trail is 2.4 miles out and back, and the Long Trail is 2.6 miles out and back.

Background, History, and Fun Facts

Mount Jo may not boast the height of the High Peaks, but it holds a special place in Adirondack lore, and in the hearts of locals and ADK hikers alike. Sitting just 2,876 feet above Heart Lake, this modest summit offers one of the most iconic views in the entire park. Standing on its summit ledge, you look out over Heart Lake with the mighty MacIntyre Range—Algonquin, Wright, and Colden—towering in the foreground. It's a view that has inspired thousands of Adirondack adventures.

The mountain was named in 1877 by Henry Van Hoevenberg, the visionary behind the Adirondack Loj. Van Hoevenberg named the peak in honor of his then fiancée, Josephine Schofield. Josephine passed away tragically (and some say suspiciously) before they could marry, leaving Henry Van Hoevenberg with a broken heart and a mountain that became her memorial. More than a century later, the mountain still bears her name.

Mount Jo sits entirely on land owned and operated by the Adirondack Mountain Club (https://adk.org). That makes it unique among Adirondack peaks, and deeply significant because this little mountain has introduced generations of hikers to the outdoors. For many people Mount Jo is often their very first hike. The Adirondack Mountain Club has recognized Mount Jo's role as a "gateway" peak, and over the years they've carefully maintained and improved its trails to balance accessibility with sustainability.

Mount Jo may be small, but it has a big story—from a tragic love tale to a conservation story, and the experiences of countless new hikers who take their first steps toward the High Peaks on its well-maintained trails.

This mountain quickly shows you all the Adirondacks have to offer.

5 Big Crow Mountain (2,815 feet)

Don't let the short mileage fool you here—Big Crow packs a punch. This mountain will make your legs and lungs work with every step for those magnificent summit views. At just 1.2 miles round-trip, this little peak delivers one of the best effort-to-view ratios in the entire Adirondacks. In less than an hour, you'll find yourself standing on an open summit ledge with outstanding views of the High Peaks, the Great Range, and Hurricane Mountain with its fire tower standing proudly to the east. It's the kind of hike locals visit over and over again.

Start: Crow's Clearing Trailhead
Elevation gain: 600 feet
Summit elevation: 2,815 feet
Distance: 1.2 miles out and back
Difficulty: 3 out of 7, moderate
Hiking time: 1.5–3 hours
Seasons: Spring, summer, fall (winter parking changes)
Fees/permits: None
Pets: All dogs must be on leash.
Trail surface: Smooth and rocky
Land status: Hurricane Mountain Wilderness
Nearest town: Keene, NY
Water availability: None
Amenities available: None
Sunrise or sunset: Sunset
Views: Excellent views of the High Peaks, Hurricane Mountain, Little Crow, and more

Finding the Trailhead: From Lake Placid, go 15 miles east on Route 73 to Keene. At 200 yards past the intersection with Route 9N in Keene, turn left on Hurricane Road at the Keene Town Hall. At just over 2 miles from Route 73, bear left onto the dirt road called O'Toole Lane and continue for 1.2 miles to the end at Crow's Clearing. The trail to Big Crow begins on the left side of the clearing. Note that the latter portion of this road is unplowed during winter. Hikers will have an additional 0.3-mile walk up the road to the trailhead. Park at your own risk along the road.
Trailhead GPS: 44.2609°N, 73.7330°W

The Hike

The trail begins at Crow's Clearing, located at the end of O'Toole Lane, a dirt road off East Hill Road in Keene. This parking area is also the trailhead for the Soda Range loop—a spectacular 6-mile ridge hike if you're looking to tack on something bigger and unique. From the trail register, the trail heads into a mixed forest. The first 0.2 mile rolls gently over rocks and some small streams, but the climbing starts quickly and abruptly.

From here, it's straight uphill to the summit. The trail is steep and rocky in places, though generally in good condition, as it climbs over 600 feet in elevation in only 0.4 mile. This small stretch rivals High Peaks hiking. Around the 0.4-mile mark you'll hit the junction with the Nun-da-ga-o Ridge (Soda Range) Trail branching off to the right. Stay left for Big Crow and keep climbing. As you gain elevation, the forest begins to thin and the trail crosses slabs of open rock. That first glimpse through the

Big Crow's perfect summit view.

trees is a preview of what's waiting above. It may feel intimidating, but just remember one foot in front of the other.

At just 0.6 mile you'll step onto Big Crow's wide-open rock summit. And what a view it is. Giant Mountain towers in the foreground, Hurricane rises to the east, and more than two dozen High Peaks stretch across the horizon. Down below, the East Branch of the Ausable River snakes through the valley. For such a short hike, the view from Big Crow feels enormous. Despite being so close to downtown Keene, this mountain offers a deep backcountry experience.

From the summit, you'll spot Little Crow down the ridge to the southwest. You can summit both in one trip by following cairns and trail markers across the open rock and along the ridgeline. If you descend Little Crow, the trail will drop you out on Hurricane Road. From there, it's a 1-mile road walk back to your car at Crow's Clearing, making for a fun thru-hike of "The Crows." Be aware that the loop is less traveled, so be vigilant to not get off trail or lost.

While steep in spots, Big Crow is a quick, family-friendly option that delivers the full Adirondack package: a short trail, a workout for the lungs and legs, and a summit view that holds its own with many of the 4,000-foot High Peaks. Big Crow is one of the most popular Lake Placid 9'ers for this reason.

Big Crow Mountain

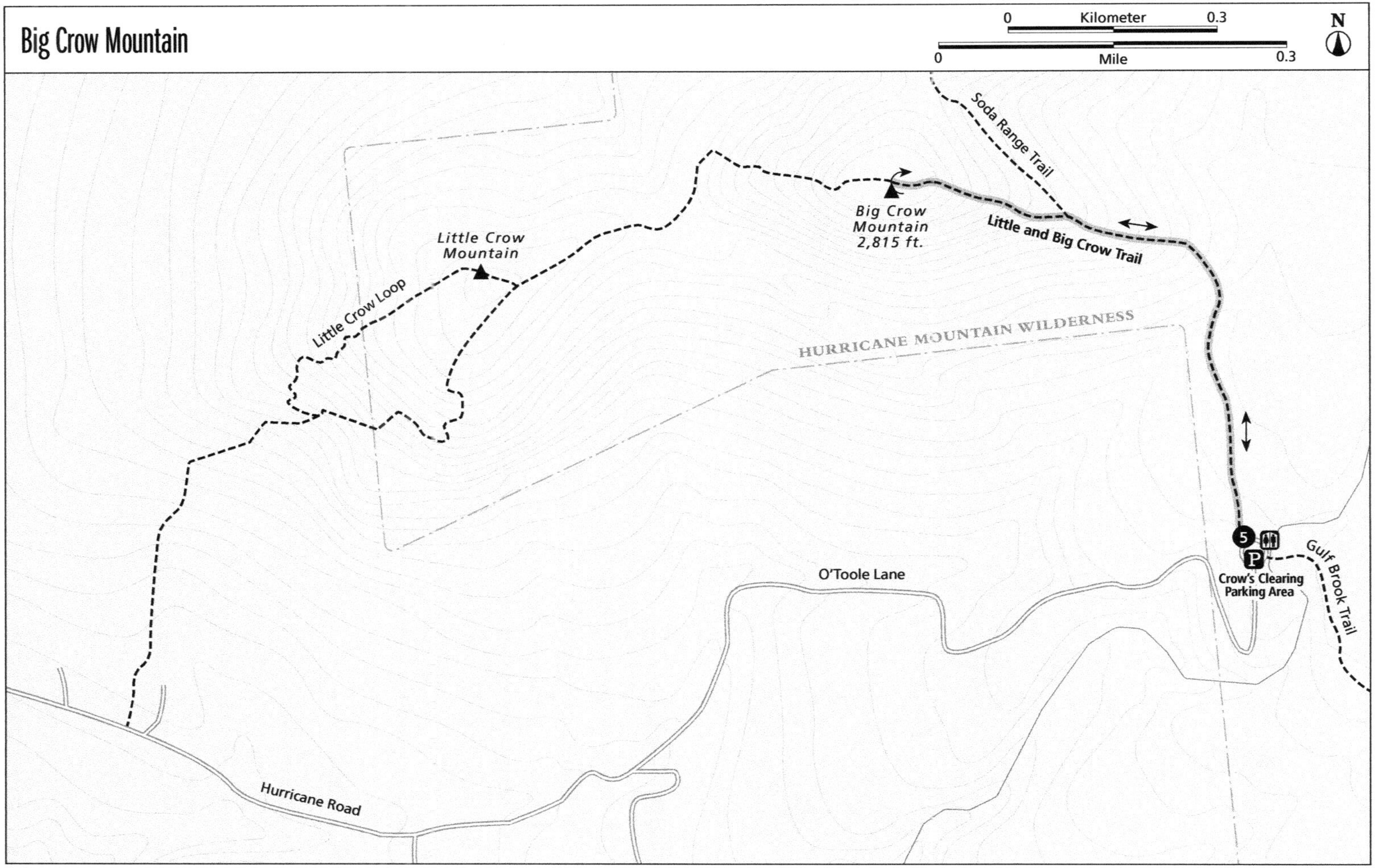

More High Peaks seen from Big Crow.

Miles and Directions

0.0 Start at the trailhead at the Crow's Clearing parking area on O'Toole Lane.

0.2 Elevation gain begins.

0.4 Stay left at the trail junction toward Big Crow Mountain; the trail to the right is the Soda Range loop, also known as the Nun-da-ga-o Ridge.

0.6 Arrive at the summit of Big Crow Mountain. Head back the way you came, or you can continue over the summit toward Little Crow to do the loop.

1.2 Arrive back at the Crow's Clearing Trailhead.

Other Routes

There are no other routes up Big Crow. This mountain can be enjoyed on its own or alongside the Soda Range (Nun-da-ga-o Ridge) or Little Crow loop. I recommend enjoying both trails on separate hikes because they're both fantastic in their own way. Be aware during the winter months that you'll hike an extra 0.3 mile up O'Toole Lane to Crow's Clearing Trailhead due to unplowed roads near the trailhead.

Background, History, and Fun Facts

Big Crow might only climb to 2,815 feet, but this little peak has a big personality. Sitting at the edge of the Hurricane Mountain Wilderness, you can see twenty-eight High Peaks from its open rock summit, making Big Crow a giant all its own. After all, not many 4,000-footers showcase over half of the 46 High Peaks, let alone a small peak in Keene like Big Crow. Counting all twenty-eight is like a parlor game that adds to the fun of the summit. If you can spot all twenty-eight, consider yourself the winner.

Giant Mountain fills the foreground of the summit view, while the Great Range stretches across the horizon, and neighboring LP9'er Hurricane Mountain stands tall with its fire tower to the east. If you squint, you'll see the fire tower. Big Crow offers the kind of summit view that makes you wonder how such a short climb can deliver such a big, High Peaks–caliber view. It's also the type of mountain that makes you wonder how such a short hike can make you sweat and breathe so heavily.

"The Crows" got their name from the early settlers of Keene, who noticed the notorious black birds circling over East Hill and gave the twin peaks their name, Big Crow and Little Crow. The name first appeared on maps in the late 1800s, and today the two summits are often hiked together as "The Crows."

The rugged Nun-da-ga-o Ridge (sometimes called the Soda Range) is also hiked from the same trail. That ridge hike is a local favorite, with a name that's as mysterious as the trail itself. Some say it's an old Abenaki word, others claim it was just a playful invention that stuck, but either way, it adds a bit of folklore to the Keene Valley skyline. It's also a fantastic hike with great views and minimal foot traffic.

Over the years, Big Crow has become a go-to hike for families, scout troops, and school groups. It's a great mountain to cut your teeth on. Keene locals often return for a quick "after-work hike" or even as a "workout hike." It's a prime example that there's more to the Adirondack Mountains than just the High Peaks and proves that sometimes the little peaks offer the biggest stories. It's a true gem here in the High Peaks region.

6 Bear Den Mountain (at Whiteface Mountain) (2,650 feet)

Bear Den Mountain (at Whiteface) is tucked right into the Whiteface Mountain Ski Resort, and it's a fun, rugged little hike with plenty of reward. The trailhead is located at the Bear Den Lot, on the north side of the parking area. From the very start, you'll feel like you're deep in the backcountry even though you're just steps from the world-famous Olympic ski mountain. The summit on Bear Den offers an unparalleled view of Whiteface Mountain worth many visits.

Start: Bear Den Lot Trailhead at Whiteface Mountain Ski Resort
Elevation gain: 1,350 feet
Summit elevation: 2,650 feet
Distance: 3.4 miles out and back
Difficulty: 4 out of 7, moderate
Hiking time: 2.5–5 hours
Seasons: All
Fees/permits: None
Pets: All dogs must be on leash.
Trail surface: Smooth
Land status: Whiteface Mountain Ski Center
Nearest town: Wilmington, NY
Water availability: None
Amenities available: Whiteface Mountain Ski Center
Sunrise or sunset: Sunrise
Views: Front-row views of Whiteface Mountain and Sentinel Range. Excellent fall foliage peak.

Finding the Trailhead: From the intersection of Route 73 and Route 86 in Lake Placid, follow Route 86 toward Wilmington. Continue for 9.2 miles to the Whiteface Mountain Ski Center. Turn into the ski center and follow the road around to the right to the Bear Den parking lot. You'll see the trailhead signs. Note that sometimes the gate on the road is closed; hikers will then have to park in an outer lot at Whiteface Mountain Ski Resort and walk down the road to the trailhead.
Trailhead GPS: 44.3595°N, 73.8576°W

The Hike

The trail begins winding across the hillside for a good half-mile warm-up through a rough, often wet section of trail. At about 0.5 mile you'll reach a trail junction with mountain biking trails. Stay left here to continue on the Bear Den Mountain Trail; straight ahead is reserved for the bike trails. From this point on, the route is a true footpath. The trail is narrower, sometimes faint, and requires paying attention to the markers. A map and compass (or GPS) are smart to bring along.

A winter sunrise from Bear Den overlooking the ski trails on Whiteface Mountain.

The first mile is fairly forgiving, but soon the elevation gain picks up and stays consistent as you climb toward the ridgeline. Around 1.6 miles the climb eases as you step onto a notch in the ridge. This is where the trail divides and you've got a choice:

1. Go left and stay in the trees a little longer before stepping out onto an open ledge with excellent views of the Sentinel Range and Whiteface close by.
2. Go right and the trail quickly turns tougher with some steeper climbing, rocky outcroppings, and eventually a short scramble near the summit. This higher northern knob is actually taller than the marked "true" summit to the south, and the scramble makes it feel like a typical ADK mountain climb.

Both directions deliver satisfying views, but if you're comfortable with steeper terrain, heading right gives you a more adventurous finish. Both are considered the summit and will deliver similar views. Going left is what most hikers do.

Miles and Directions

0.0 Arrive at the Whiteface Mountain Ski Resort Bear Den parking lot. Look for the trailhead register.

0.5 Take the left trail to the summit of Bear Den Mountain.

Bear Den Mountain (at Whiteface Mountain)

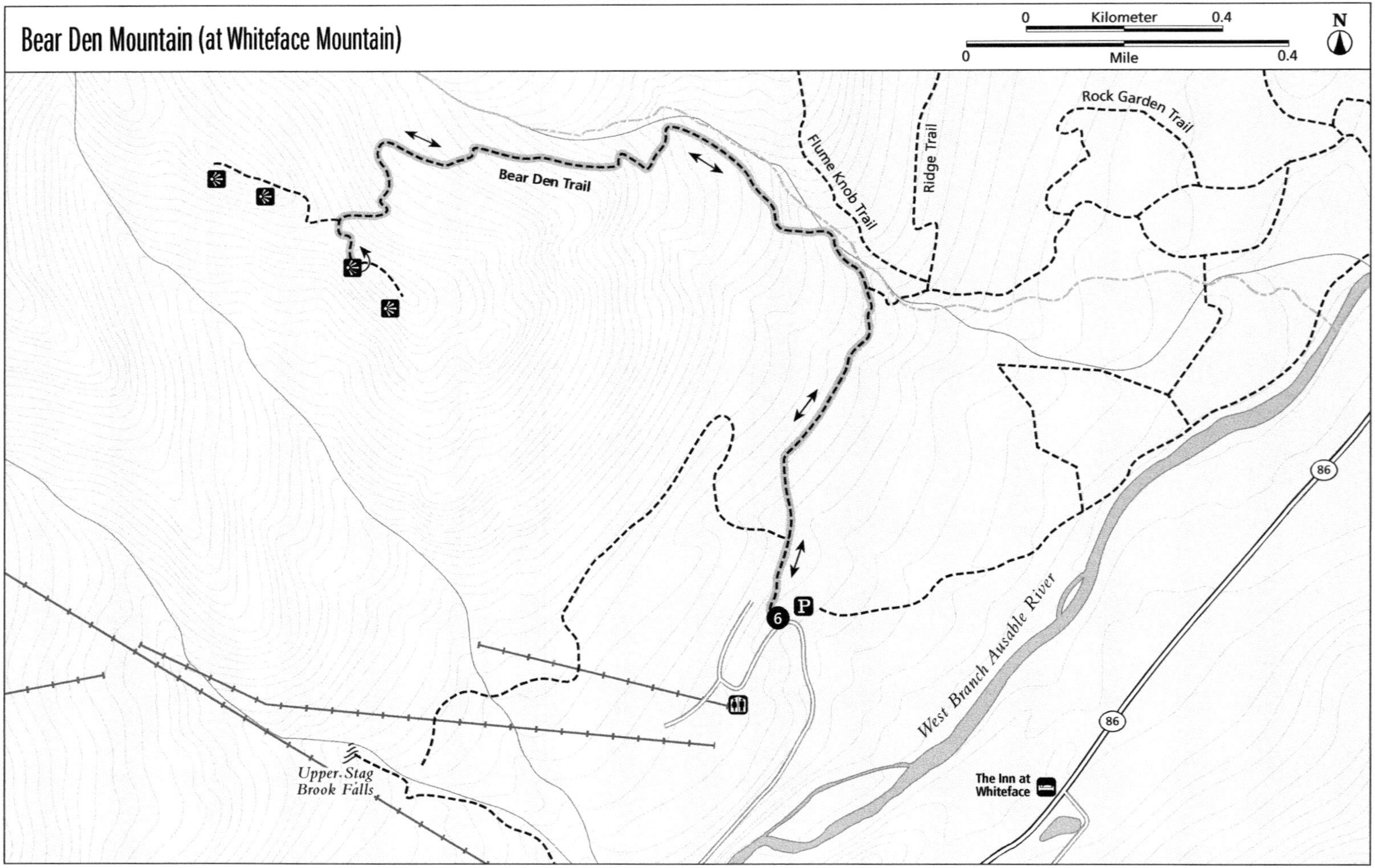

1.6 The trail starts to become steeper as you hike the crest of the ridge. I recommend going left here.

1.7 Arrive at the summit where unparalleled views of Whiteface Mountain await. The MacIntyre Range and other High Peaks lie in the distance. Hike back down the way you came up.

3.4 Arrive back at the trailhead parking lot.

Other Routes

There are no other routes up Bear Den Mountain. Note the two summit options. Both are valid and offer similar views.

Background, History, and Fun Facts

Bear Den stands on its own when it comes to hiking, but it's the little brother of next-door neighbor Whiteface Mountain, offering a perfect blend of classic Adirondack hiking and the Adirondack Olympic legacy.

Whiteface Mountain is undoubtedly the star of the region. At 4,867 feet, it's one of the tallest mountains in New York and was home to the alpine ski events during the 1980 Winter Olympics. Over 200,000 skiers and snowboarders carve down its slopes every winter. With the greatest vertical drop east of the Rockies (3,430 feet), its Olympic legacy, and the Veterans Memorial Highway leading nearly to its summit, Whiteface Mountain is one of the most storied peaks in the ADK. Bear Den gives you a front-row view to it all.

Bear Den also sits in the middle of two worlds. While the world of Whiteface sits to its west, on the east side of the mountain lies another world—the Wilmington Wild Forest. The Flume Trail System here is a network of both hiking and mountain bike trails that wind along the West Branch of the Ausable River.

And speaking of rivers, just minutes up the road you'll find popular staples of the Ausable River in the Flume swimming holes and High Falls Gorge, making this area one of the most adventure-rich corners of the Adirondacks.

7 Pitchoff Mountain (3,497 feet)

Pitchoff Mountain is a long, rugged mountain in the Sentinel Range that sits right across Route 73 from the popular Cascade Mountain Trailhead. At nearly 3,500 feet, it's the eightieth-tallest peak in the Adirondacks and hikes like a High Peak. Pitchoff delivers a full-value Adirondack adventure. With ledges, scrambles, and scattered views throughout, this trail has everything a hiker would want in an Adirondack hiking adventure.

Start: Pitchoff Trailhead (Route 73)
Elevation gain: 1,410 feet
Summit elevation: 3,497 feet
Distance: 4.8 miles out and back (West Trail) / 5.9 miles point to point (East Trail)
Difficulty: 5 out of 7, hard
Hiking time: 3–5 hours
Seasons: All
Fees/permits: None
Pets: All dogs must be on leash.
Trail surface: Smooth and rocky
Land status: Sentinel Range Wilderness
Nearest town: Lake Placid, NY
Water availability: None
Amenities available: None
Sunrise or sunset: Sunset
Views: Wooded summit. Excellent views of Cascade Mountain and the Cascade Lakes from Balanced Rocks lookout.

Finding the Trailhead: From the intersection of Route 73 and Route 86 in Lake Placid, follow Route 73 toward Keene. Continue on Route 73 for 7.5 miles to the Pitchoff West Trail. For Pitchoff East Trail, continue 2.7 miles farther on Route 73. Both trailheads are on the left, but parking is along the right shoulder for the East trailhead. Be careful when crossing this busy road. **Trailhead GPS:** 44.21917°N, 73.88694°W

The Hike

There are two main ways to hike Pitchoff: the West Trail from the Cascade/Pitchoff parking area or the East Trail on the opposite end of the Cascade Lakes toward Keene. You can hike it out and back from either end, but many hikers prefer to make it a traverse along the entire 5.9-mile ridge. If you go that route, you'll need two cars. Walking back along Route 73 is dangerous and not recommended.

From the western trailhead, the climb starts steep right out of the gate, rising quickly above Route 73. The trail passes a few outlooks over Upper and Lower Cascade Lakes before tackling a rockier stretch. At about 1.5 miles you'll reach the trail junction sign to Balanced Rocks. Balanced Rocks is the place with big views to sit and enjoy your snack and summit sandwich on this mountain. It can be visited on the way up or down the mountain.

As its name suggests, Balanced Rocks is exactly what it sounds like: a group of massive boulders perched on the edge of a wide-open slab. The view here is one of

Cascade Mountain and the Cascade Lakes from Pitchoff. JONATHAN ZAHAREK

Five-year-old Penny Jean enjoying a mid-hike snack on Pitchoff.

the best in the entire High Peaks region. Cascade rises directly across the valley, Giant and Hurricane stand tall in the distance, and you can even spot the Olympic bobsled track far to the right. On a clear day you'll see more than a dozen High Peaks lined up in the sky. Most hikers consider Balanced Rocks the true highlight of Pitchoff.

Continuing from the Balanced Rocks junction, the trail works its way along Pitchoff's narrow ridgeline. At 2.4 miles you'll reach the wooded true summit of Pitchoff, marked by a boulder and a small cairn. There isn't much of a view here; the best outlooks are either still ahead if continuing on the traverse, or back at Balanced Rocks.

If traversing along the Pitchoff East Trail: Expect plenty of ups and downs as you climb over a series of subpeaks, squeeze between boulders, and scramble across rocky slabs. The ridge walk is classic Adirondacks filled with roots, ledges, and big views that seem to pop up every half mile. Subpeaks along the ridge provide stunning perspectives of the Great Range, Giant, Hurricane, Whiteface, and even the Olympic Jumping Complex in Lake Placid. The north summit, at 3,323 feet, is especially impressive with nearly 360-degree views.

From this summit area the trail begins its long descent toward the eastern trailhead. This section is steep and eroded in places, with a few tricky scrambles, stream crossings, and muddy stretches. The footing can be tough, but as the trail levels out near Route 73, it gives way to easier walking before arriving at the Pitchoff East Trailhead.

If you're looking for a trail less traveled that will get your heart, legs, and lungs working, the Pitchoff East Trail up to the first summit is a great short, quick, steep hike with big views.

Penny Jean enjoying a hike with her dad up the Pitchoff East Trail.

One of Pitchoff's most famous spots is Balanced Rocks. These massive boulders, known as glacial erratics, look like they were dropped onto the mountainside by giants. Glacial erratics—which are all over the mountains—are rocks carried and deposited by retreating glaciers thousands of years ago. As the last ice age ended, glaciers moved huge slabs of rock before leaving them behind in places that seem almost impossible, which is why they're fun to look at. Balanced Rocks is one of those places. Standing beneath and on Balanced Rocks, with Cascade Pass opening in front of you below, it's hard not to feel humbled by the scale of nature, geology, and time.

Pitchoff is another local staple. It may sit just across Route 73 from the busiest trailhead in the Adirondacks, but the Pitchoff trail will take you into another world entirely.

My hiking partner, Josh Bliss, having fun at Balanced Rocks on Pitchoff.

8 Hurricane Mountain (3,678 feet)

Hurricane Mountain is one of the true gems of the Adirondacks and the Lake Placid 9. Its wide, open summit is highlighted by a fully restored fire tower, along with one of the best near-360-degree views in the Adirondacks. From the top you'll see the High Peaks to the west, Lake Champlain stretching to the east, and the Green Mountains of Vermont in the distance. There are a few different trail options for Hurricane, but my recommendation is the Route 9N southern approach trail. At 3,678 feet, it's not a High Peak, but Hurricane hikes like one and offers everything the High Peaks offer. Anytime someone visits the Adirondacks and asks me what mountain they should hike, I always send them to Hurricane Mountain. Yes, it's that good.

Start: Route 9N Trailhead (Southern Approach)
Elevation gain: 1,986 feet
Summit elevation: 3,678 feet
Distance: 6.8 miles out and back
Difficulty: 5 out of 7, hard
Hiking time: 3–6 hours
Seasons: All
Fees/permits: None
Pets: All dogs must be on leash.
Trail surface: Smooth and rocky
Land status: Hurricane Mountain Wilderness
Nearest town: Keene, NY, and Elizabethtown, NY
Water availability: Light streams
Amenities available: None
Sunrise or sunset: Both
Views: Unbeatable views of the High Peaks with a fire tower

Finding the Trailhead: Route 9N Trailhead (Southern Approach): Take Route 73 east from Lake Placid and turn left onto Route 9N after 15.5 miles. The parking area is 3.5 miles up the road on both sides. The trailhead is on the left. **Trailhead GPS:** 44.21139°N, 73.72306°W

Crow's Clearing Trailhead (Northern Approach): From Lake Placid, go 15 miles east on Route 73 to Keene. At 200 yards past the intersection with Route 9N in Keene, turn left on Hurricane Road at the Keene Town Hall. At just over 2 miles from Route 73, bear left onto the dirt road called O'Toole Lane and continue for 1.2 miles to the end at Crow's Clearing. The trail to Big Crow begins on the left side of the clearing. Note that the latter portion of this road is unplowed during winter. Hikers will have an additional 0.3-mile walk up the road to the trailhead. **Trailhead GPS:** 44.2609°N, 73.7330°W

The Hike

Route 9N (Southern Approach)

From the trailhead parking on Route 9N, the trail begins climbing right away. It then levels briefly before crossing a long boardwalk through a marshy bog with views of Green Mountain (3,980 feet) above. After crossing a small stream, the climbing begins again. The climb is steady but never overwhelming, on a good trail through a mix of hardwoods and evergreens.

Hurricane Mountain summit.

Sunrise on Hurricane Mountain.

By 2.0 miles in, the trail has gained plenty of elevation, but some well-built switchbacks make the elevation gain feel reasonable. Soon the climb steepens again, and at 3.0 miles you'll step out onto open rock slabs with your first big look at the summit fire tower.

At 3.2 miles the trail meets the junction with the route from Crow's Clearing. Stay right, and soon you'll break out onto the bald summit. From here the fire tower stands at the far end of the open ridge. The views stretch in every direction—Giant and the Great Range to the southwest, Mount Marcy on the far horizon, and eastward over Lake Champlain to Vermont's Green Mountains. It's one of the most complete panoramas in the park. This mountain is also called Hurricane for a reason—the wind is likely to whipping.

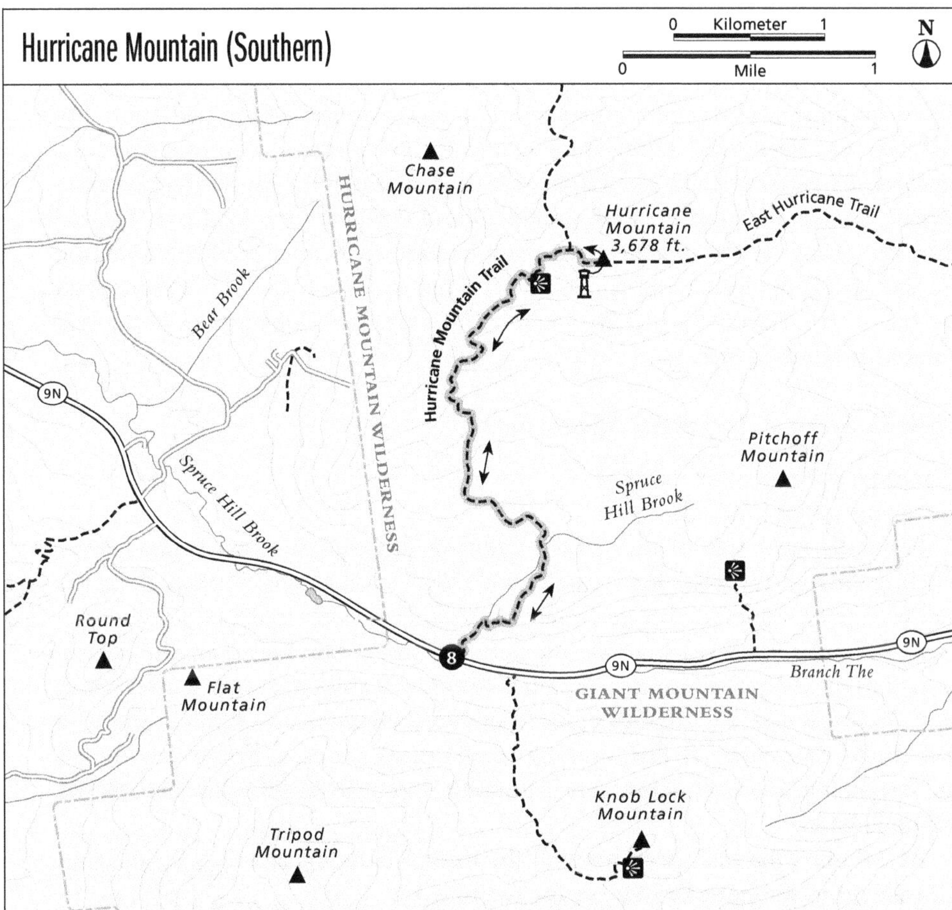

From the gate, hike 1.2 miles up the road to the site of the old observer's cabin. From there, the trail drops down to a stream before climbing back up to another stream at around 1.4 miles. Once passing the second stream, it's a steep climb all the way to the summit. Your legs and lungs will definitely work for this one.

Background, History, and Fun Facts

Hurricane is a fan-favorite for LP9 hikers for myriad reasons, one of them being it's the only mountain in the challenge with a fire tower. Fire towers are a staple of Adirondack history. There's even another popular hiking challenge called the ADK Fire Tower Challenge that includes hiking at least eighteen of the twenty-three Adirondack mountains with fire towers, and all five Catskills peaks with fire towers (visit https://adk.org for information).

Hurricane's fire tower has been standing since 1919, when the state installed a 35-foot steel structure to improve fire detection after a series of devastating wildfires swept the area. Before that, observers sat right on the open cliffs with nothing more than a telephone line strung down the mountain.

Today the tower is fully restored and open to climb, complete with a mountain map inside pointing out peaks in every direction. While standing up there, you can almost picture what it was like for the early observers scanning the horizon looking for signs of smoke. Incredible to think that the view you're looking at is the same view they were looking at. It's a view that never gets old.

9 Catamount Mountain (3,169 feet)

Catamount sits northeast of Whiteface and Wilmington, offering one of the most rewarding and unexpected summits in the Whiteface region. Its open false summit and true summit, steep rock slabs, and the "chimney" scramble give hikers something different from the other Lake Placid 9'er peaks. Something more challenging. A mountain that requires more focus than the rest. Catamount truly prepares hikers for what they'll experience out in the High Peaks.

Catamount is one of those hikes that feels bigger than it looks on paper. As you drive up to this lone peak, you'll see it towering in the sky in the most majestic way. Sitting at 2.0 miles one-way, this rugged little peak in the Wilmington Wild Forest delivers everything you'd want in an Adirondack hike.

It's not a High Peak, but it hikes like one. Many hikers consider it one of the most fun "low peaks" in the Adirondacks—especially if you like to use your hands on the way up. This is arguably the most challenging hike of the Lake Placid 9 and is best saved for last. Once you can successfully and confidently summit Catamount, I believe you're ready for the 46 High Peaks.

Start: Catamount Trailhead on Plank Road/ Forestdale Road
Elevation gain: 1,545 feet
Summit elevation: 3,169 feet
Distance: 4.0 miles out and back
Difficulty: 5 out of 7, hard
Hiking time: 2.5–5 hours
Seasons: All
Fees/permits: None
Pets: All dogs must be on leash.
Trail surface: Smooth and rocky
Land status: Wilmington Wild Forest
Nearest town: Wilmington, NY
Water availability: Light brook
Amenities available: None
Sunrise or sunset: Both
Views: Full 360-degree views of Whiteface, Esther, McKenzie, Moose, and many more

Finding the Trailhead: From the four-corner intersection in the village of Wilmington, head west up Route 431. At the intersection with the Whiteface Memorial Highway, just before the toll house, bear right toward Franklin Falls (CR 72 or Gillespie Drive on some maps). Continue for 3.3 miles to Roseman Road and take a right. Follow Roseman Road for 0.8 mile and turn right on Plank Road. Follow that for 2.2 miles, to the parking area on the left. Note there is no cell phone service at this trailhead. **Trailhead GPS:** 44.4431°N, 73.8799°W

The Hike

From the trailhead and register near the parking area, the hike starts nice and easy. The first half mile winds on a flat, broad path through a mix of wildflowers, moss, and hardwoods. The trail runs along private property so be extra respectful and stay on the trail. At 0.6 mile the path bears right, then dips to cross a brook at 0.8 mile.

Driving up to Catamount Mountain's trailhead—a stunning view.

Once across the brook, the real climbing begins. The trail steepens steadily, working its way through birches and across rock-strewn pitches until, at 1.4 miles, you reach Catamount's signature feature: a narrow, 20-foot rock chimney. This is the challenging (and fun!) part. Expect to use your hands and strength to climb up. Small children, dogs, and anyone not comfortable with heights or small climbs may struggle here. Some dogs may need help from their owners. Once above the chimney, wrap around to the left and look for the next trail marker.

Just above the chimney, the mountain opens up as you arrive on the false summit. Enjoy sweeping views before going over and back in the woods toward the summit. This trail can be confusing at times, so it's important to stay vigilant looking for trail markers. When on the rock slabs, follow the yellow blazes (some are fading) and the rock cairns (piles of rocks acting as trail markers) carefully. Route-finding can be tricky on open slabs anywhere, and this mountain is no exception.

Slab climbing on Catamount. JONATHAN ZAHAREK

At 1.8 miles, more views of Whiteface with its Veterans Memorial Highway and castle-like summit building are clearly visible. The building on the summit of Whiteface is a weather observatory.

The final 0.5 mile is a mix of open rock scrambles and ledges. Just remember when climbing that it's important to always keep three points of contact—either two feet and one hand, or two hands and one foot.

At 2.7 miles you'll crest the true summit, marked by a benchmark on a rocky hump in a clearing of low trees. It's not completely open, but walk a few steps in any direction and you'll find a different view. To the southwest is Whiteface and Esther, then to the east you'll see the Green Mountains of Vermont (Mount Mansfield and Camel's Hump). To the northwest, Silver Lake and Union Falls Pond shine below,

Catamount Mountain

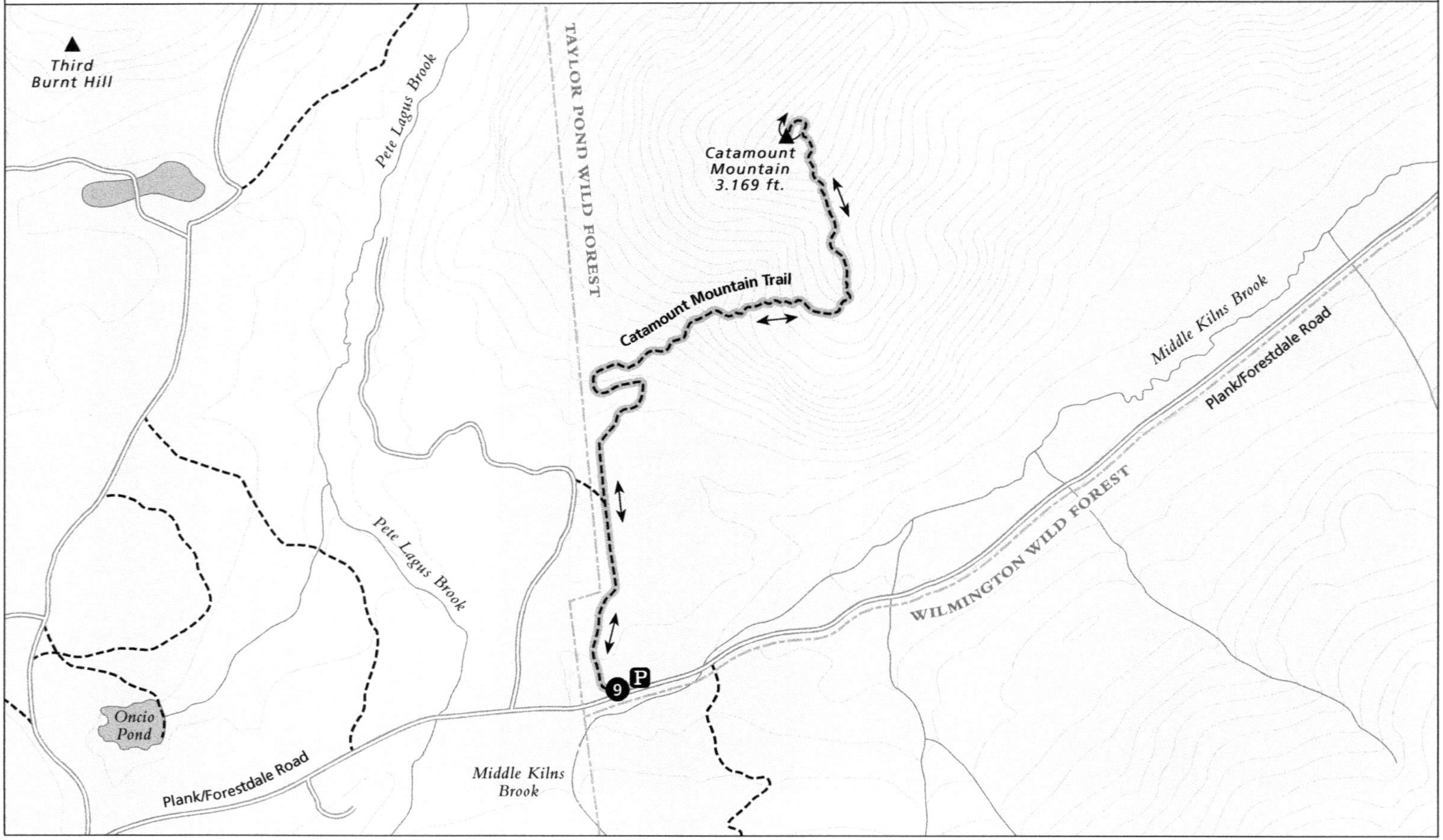

along with views that take the eye to the edge of the world. If you can handle the inevitable bugs, this summit is worth an extended stay.

On the descent be vigilant about looking for trail markers, and don't be afraid to take some extra time to search for them if you're not confident. Herd paths form from people missing markers, which adds to the confusion. So be focused on the way down. It's worth noting that this mountain can be slick and extra challenging in wet conditions. Be cautious if hiking on a wet day, and don't be afraid to turn around if need be. The mountain will always be there.

Miles and Directions

0.0 Start at the trailhead at the corner of the parking lot.

0.8 Cross an unreliable streamlet on a footbridge.

1.4 Climb up the rock chimney.

1.5 Arrive on a false summit; the true summit towers above.

1.6 Clear view of Whiteface Mountain.

1.7 Begin the final rock scramble, following blazes and cairns.

2.0 Arrive at the summit and enjoy wonderful views from all sides. Head back down the way you came up. Be cautious and focused on the descent.

4.0 Arrive back at the parking lot.

Other Routes

There are no other routes up Catamount Mountain.

Background, History, and Fun Facts

The name "Catamount" has been around since at least 1868, appearing on W. W. Ely's famous *Map of the New York Wilderness*. "Catamount" is just another word for mountain lion or cougar. There's no official record of big cats prowling these ridges today, and the DEC claims there is no evidence of their existence ever in the Adirondacks. People claim to have seen them in the past, which makes the lore of it all more fun. The nineteenth-century Great Adirondack surveyor, Verplanck Colvin, once referred to the mountain as Thi-pac Mountain, but as maps evolved, "Catamount" stuck.

The trail to Catamount has not always been easy to find and as official as it now seems when you arrive at the trailhead parking. A few decades ago, there was barely a proper parking lot, just small cairns marking the trailhead on back roads. As interest grew, so did the infrastructure for this adventurous mountain.

What makes Catamount so memorable among hikers' Lake Placid 9'er journey is, without question, "the chimney." The chimney on Catamount is a rite-of-passage moment during the LP9. It's a brief, narrow rock crack in the mountain—the type of spot hikers love (or fear) but ultimately adds character. It's steep, requires some

Climbing the Catamount chimney. JONATHAN ZAHAREK

The Catamount chimney on a perfect winter day.

care, and gives a taste of what scrambling feels like without pushing into technical terrain. It may be the most memorable 20-yard stretch of trail on the Lake Placid 9.

Catamount flies under the radar compared to the High Peaks, but that's part of its charm and allure. It's less crowded, surprisingly rugged, unexpectedly scenic, and a great Adirondack Mountain challenge. Catamount prepares hikers for the 46 High Peaks in a truly authentic way.

Preparing for the Uncontrollables

Hiking mountains (or any other outdoor activity) comes with a lot of factors outside our control—weather conditions, trail conditions, other people, wildlife, and so on. It's important to be prepared for these uncontrollable elements. It's equally important to control what you can control, such as your physical preparation, gear, food, water, knowledge of the trail, looking at the weather forecast, and more. As hikers it's our responsibility to control what we can control and be prepared for what we can't control. The mountains do not care about you, so please plan accordingly.

Severe Weather

If there's one thing you learn quickly in the Adirondacks, it's that the weather makes its own rules. The forecast on your phone might say sunshine all day, but the mountains might have different plans. I've been pelted with hail in July and hiked through pouring rain in February. Up here, the calendar doesn't always matter and the weather report doesn't always hold up, because the mountains will do what they want. They are in charge.

That's why you always need to be prepared for anything. A clear, sunny morning at the trailhead can turn into cold wind and driving rain by the time you reach the summit. Temperatures at the top are usually 10 to 20 degrees cooler than down below, and if you're wet and exposed, that's a recipe for trouble. Hypothermia doesn't just happen in the dead of winter either; it can set in on a cool summer evening if you're soaked through and unprepared.

The solution is simple: respect the mountains and prepare for "uncontrollables" like the weather. Keep a rain jacket in your pack every season of the year, even when the forecast promises blue skies. Throw in an extra mid-layer—yes, even in summer—so you've got something warm when the wind picks up. A little extra weight in your pack is a small price to pay for staying safe and dry.

The Adirondacks are as lush and green as they are for a reason—it rains a lot. That's part of the magic of this place. Just make sure you head into every hike knowing that the mountains don't care about predicted forecasts, and they certainly don't care about your plans. Be ready for whatever they throw your way, and you'll set yourself up for a safe and memorable day on the trail.

"Warning: Weather Subject to Severe Change"

The title of this section is seen on signs all around the Adirondack Mountains, and for good reason. Few things will humble you in the mountains like a thunderstorm rolling in out of nowhere. One minute it's bluebird skies, the next it's dark clouds, wind, and the sound of thunder echoing off the peaks. Storms build fast in the mountains and move even faster.

That's why timing matters. This is what I mean by "preparing for the uncontrollable": While your gear, preparation, and attitude are all within your control, the weather is not. So it's important to be prepared for it.

Most summer thunderstorms pop up in the afternoon, which is another reason I always recommend starting your hikes early. The earlier you hit the trail, the earlier you're off the summits and back below the tree line, before storms start cooking.

If the forecast is calling for thunderstorms, it's best to skip the bigger mountains altogether. The Adirondacks are full of shorter hikes, waterfalls, and forest trails that are perfect options on stormy days. But sometimes, no matter what the forecast says, a storm will still find you. I've been caught before on peaks when the skies turned on me with little warning—it happens.

If it does, your priority is simple: Get down from exposed areas as quickly and safely as possible. Summits, ridgelines, and open ledges are the last places you want to be. Get back into the trees, and spread out if you're with a group until the storm passes.

Remember what your mom always told you: Make good decisions. Once again, the mountains will always be there tomorrow.

Orphaning a Peak: Live to Hike Another Day

One of the hardest lessons hikers learn in the Adirondacks is that sometimes you have to turn around. In the hiking world we call this "orphaning" a peak. It simply means you didn't make the summit because you had to turn around and abandon the mission. And that's okay—it happens to all of us.

It can sting in the moment because you've put in the miles, you've climbed the elevation, you're right there. But truthfully, no mountain is worth risking your safety for. Bad weather, slick conditions, fading daylight, not feeling right—whatever the reason—turning back is always the right call if conditions aren't safe or you're "just not feeling it" that day. The mountains aren't going anywhere, but you need to make sure you do.

Every seasoned hiker has orphaned peaks at one time or another for various reasons. It's part of the game. The longer you spend in the mountains, the more at peace you'll become with the idea. A little frustration today is a lot better than an injury, an unplanned overnight, or worse.

Do yourself, your loved ones, and the DEC forest rangers who may have to come looking for you a favor: Respect the conditions and live to hike another day. That summit will still be there next time.

Shoulder Seasons: Spring/Fall at the Trailhead, Winter at the Summit

If you spend enough time hiking in the Adirondacks, you'll quickly learn that the season at the trailhead isn't always the same season at the summit. Many times, I've laced up my boots for a spring hike complete with green woods, warm sun, and birds chirping, only to find myself trudging through old snow and ice an hour later.

This is the reality of shoulder season hiking. In April and May, and again in October and November, the trailhead may look and feel like late spring or fall. But as you climb higher in elevation, the season may change. It's not unusual to start in a T-shirt at the bottom and need snowshoes near the top.

The lesson is simple: Don't let the calendar fool you. Always prepare for both seasons when you head out in the spring or fall. Pack layers and traction, and be ready to switch from "summer hiking" mode back into "winter hiking" mode mid-trail.

It might feel odd to carry snow gear when the grass is green at your car, but in shoulder seasons that's the way it is. Fortunately, most of the LP9 mountains dry out faster than the High Peaks and make for great shoulder season hikes. The bigger mountains like Hurricane, Pitchoff, and Catamount, however, will have snow sooner/longer than the small peaks like Baxter, Jo, Cobble, Bear Den, or Van Hoevenberg. Plan accordingly and always be prepared.

Rain and the LP9

If you hike enough in the Adirondacks, sooner or later you will end up hiking in the rain. It's almost impossible to avoid. And while nothing beats a bluebird Adirondack day, rainy days carry their own kind of magic too. From the mist in the valleys, to the smell of wet trees, to the fact that you're literally inside the clouds, there's beauty in the misery if you look for it.

There's an old saying in the hiking world: "There's no such thing as bad weather, just the wrong clothes." This is true. A rainy day on the trail isn't so bad when you have a raincoat, hat, and the right shoes for muddy conditions. It actually has a unique charm.

That being said, some mountains are best saved for dry conditions. While all the Lake Placid 9 have grand views worth countless visits, some peaks should be avoided in the rain if possible because of slippery hiking conditions on steep slabs. Specifically, I'd recommend saving Catamount and Big Crow for dry days due to climbing on slabs.

When the weather turns, don't force a hike, but also don't let weather scare you away from hiking. The Adirondack Mountains always have a story to tell and a lesson to teach on every mountain in all conditions.

Winter Hiking

Winter has a way of stretching far past the calendar in the ADK. Locals joke about "false spring" in April, when the snow melts for a week, the sun comes out, and everyone thinks it's over only for another snowstorm (or two) to roll in a few days later.

Snow in the High Peaks and higher-elevation mountains like Hurricane, Pitchoff, and Catamount can start showing up as early as mid-September and often hangs on until June. That's why hikers carry traction and layers the majority of the year. In fact, a warm morning in May at the trailhead can sometime turn into knee-deep snow near the summit in the High Peaks. If you're not prepared, it can go from uncomfortable to dangerous in a hurry.

Winter hiking is its own world, plain and simple. The trails are buried, the trees are covered in Dr. Seuss–like fluffy snow, and the mountains feel silent in a way they never do in summer. It's stunning, but it's also unforgiving at times. A winter hike demands different gear, different preparation, and a different mindset altogether. If you're not willing to invest in the right equipment and skills, winter hiking isn't for you. The mountains need to be respected even more in the winter because mistakes in the cold can turn fatal in minutes—a harsh but undeniable reality.

Here's the good news: The Lake Placid 9'er is the perfect list of mountains to try winter hiking. Due to their lower elevation and shorter distances, you can dial in your equipment and learn the ropes under lighter conditions and on lower-consequence mountains compared to the High Peaks. So if you're new to winter hiking and want to experience the winter magic, I recommend hiking the LP9 in the order listed in this book, where each peak builds on the last. Your ability, knowledge, experience, and confidence in winter conditions will grow with every mountain.

While winter hiking does have more consequences if things go wrong—and requires more preparation than summer hiking—it's easier on the body, softer on the joints, and the views are even more stunning than the summer. You'll see!

Traction: Snowshoes and Microspikes

If there's one piece of gear I recommend keeping in your pack the majority of the year when hiking in the Adirondacks, it's microspikes. From October through June—and sometimes even in September—you'll run into icy stretches on the trail. Without traction, those slick ledges and frozen slabs can go from tricky to dangerous fast. I've had plenty of hikes where I thought to myself: *There's no way down this section without spikes on*. I've done many hikes where I never expected to need spikes, but I did. And I've done many hikes where I expected to use them, but I didn't. It's better to always be prepared even if it means a little extra weight in your pack.

The key is to make sure you've got microspikes built for the mountains. There's a big difference between the kind designed for walking the dog on an icy sidewalk and the ones made for climbing mountains. Look for sturdy chains, strong teeth, and the right size for your boot.

Snowshoes are required per the DEC when the snowpack is 8 inches or more, which is basically December through March. They might feel clunky at first, but you'll quickly find your "snow legs." Snowshoes can be rented at many local outfitters and shops around Lake Placid.

Outside of winter you may not need traction on the LP9 mountains as often as you do in the High Peaks, but the day you do need them, you'll be glad they're in your backpack—and on your feet!

Layers and Staying Warm

If traction keeps you on your feet, layers keep you alive. The Adirondacks are famous for wild swings in temperature. What feels like a crisp fall morning at the trailhead can be below freezing by the time you reach the summit. On average, expect it to be 10 to 20 degrees colder at the top, and that's before you factor in the wind.

That's why I always recommend bringing more than you think you'll need. A mid-layer fleece, an insulating "puffy" (800-fill is a good sweet spot), and a shell to block wind and rain should be staples in your pack. Yes, even in the summer. You might feel silly carrying a jacket when it's 75°F at the car, but you won't feel silly when the wind is whipping across an open summit and the temperature has dropped.

Think in terms of systems:

- **Base layer—**wicks sweat and keeps you dry
- **Mid-layer—**traps heat and keeps you warm
- **Shell layer—**shields you from wind and rain

Swap layers in and out as your body and the weather changes. With experience you'll develop the rhythm that works for you. The right clothing can make all the difference between a comfortable day on the trail and a miserable one.

Remember the mountains don't care if you're cold—they'll continue doing what they do. So do yourself a favor and pack the extra layer and bring the winter hat and the light gloves. You'll thank yourself when you're standing on the summit warm, dry, and comfortable as you enjoy your summit sandwich with a view instead of shivering.

Fitness and Physical Preparation

Hiking in the Adirondacks and beyond is all about being fully prepared—controlling what you can and being ready for what you can't. You can control your gear. You can control your knowledge of the trail, your preparation, your layers, your traction, and the food and water you carry. You can also control your attitude in the mountains, which is critical because life can get hard in the backcountry. Those things are on you, and the more dialed in you keep them, the better your chances of having a safe, successful hike.

What you can't control are the mountains themselves. The weather will do what it wants. A bluebird morning can turn into a storm by the afternoon. Trails get muddy, winds whip across the summits, snow and ice can show up in September or May. That's just life in the mountains.

The good news is, when you control the controllables and prepare for the uncontrollables, you set yourself up for a safe, successful, and fulfilling mountain adventure.

And while gear and preparation go a long way, there's one more controllable you can't overlook—your body. The stronger, fitter, and more physically prepared you are, the more enjoyable every mile becomes. Which means it's time to shift gears from what's in your pack to what's in your legs and lungs.

Training that translates to hiking mountains. JONATHAN ZAHAREK

At the end of the day, no piece of gear matters more than the body carrying it. You can have the best boots, the latest pack, and every gadget in the world, but if your legs and lungs aren't ready for the climb, the mountain will remind you quickly. Fitness is the one controllable that directly shapes how much you enjoy the journey. The stronger and physically better prepared you are, the more fulfilling the adventure becomes.

If you're new to hiking or the Adirondacks, I strongly recommend hiking the Lake Placid 9 in the order I've laid out. Each mountain was chosen to build on the last, gradually increasing in difficulty and preparing you for bigger challenges down the road. Think of it as a training plan built into the mountains: Start small, gain confidence, and keep stacking wins as you experience one summit at a time.

That steady progression, paired with attention to your physical preparation off the trail, will give you the ability to confidently enjoy every step instead of "just getting through" the hike. When your legs and lungs are prepared, hiking becomes less of a struggle and feels like the adventure it should be. That's the sweet spot we're aiming for.

At the end of the day, the engine getting you up the mountain is you. The gear in your pack doesn't matter if your legs and lungs can't take you to the summit. Take care of your body, and the mountains will reward you with an adventure you'll remember for a lifetime.

Training Beyond the Trail

For many people, simply hiking the Lake Placid 9 in order is enough to build the ability, skills, and confidence they need to move onto the bigger peaks. But for those who want to go above and beyond—who want to show up at the first trailhead stronger, fitter, and more prepared than ever—training off the trail is a game-changer. Plus, being fit for the mountains will make everything else in life a lot easier too. Fitness is fitness, right?

That's what my "Mountain-Strength Method" is all about: building strength, conditioning, and resilience that translates seamlessly into mountain adventures. The more prepared you are before you arrive at the trailhead, the more fun and rewarding the miles become. Suffering through hikes is never fun.

Here's a simple weekly framework I've used to coach hundreds of hikers all around the world to become stronger, fitter, more resilient hikers, backpackers, and people. Now you can follow it too, if you want to start improving your mountain fitness before you hit the trail.

The Mountain-Strength Method

2 Strength Sessions (45–60 minutes each)

Let strength training be your foundation. Focus on lifting weights doing functional movements: squats, leg press machine, lunges, step-ups, deadlifts, bench press, push-ups, shoulder press, rows, etc. Train with heavier weights to build strength in your muscles and joints, and keep your body resilient. No more light weight for lots of reps. Instead, aim to do 3–4 sets of each exercise lifting 5–10 reps with a challenging weight. The strength, conditioning, and muscular endurance you build will carry over to elevation gains and keep your body safer out there.

1–2 Conditioning Sessions (20–40 minutes each)
Mix in one high-intensity interval training session (think bodyweight or dumbbell circuit workouts) and one general steady-state cardio session (run, fast walk, ruck, stair climber, cycling, elliptical, etc.) a week to improve your trail endurance for elevation climbs and long miles.

1 Ruck (30–60 minutes)
Put on your loaded hiking pack and go for a "ruck" (a fast walk wearing a fully loaded backpack) in your neighborhood or on your local trails. The goal is to put in time on your feet wearing a loaded backpack, which will condition your body for the trail.

That's it. Four or five intentional and well-rounded workouts a week, scaled to your ability and built around movements that translate in the mountains. Over time, this builds not just hiking fitness, but also the kind of all-around strength and conditioning that makes life outside the gym and trail better too.

The Lake Placid 9 was designed to prepare you step by step for bigger hikes. When you pair it with a structured approach to physical fitness, you'll discover what hiking is supposed to feel like—hard, yes, but also joyful, empowering, and unforgettable.

Stronger legs hike farther in the mountains. JONATHAN ZAHAREK

in mind the old saying "be bold, start cold" applies well. Start cold, because once you get moving, you'll warm right up.

So we closed the van door, clicked on our headlamps, and began hiking up the snow-covered dirt road to the Crow's Clearing Trailhead. There were many frozen tracks in the ground, and since it hadn't snowed for a few days, there was no need today for snowshoes, though we had them on our packs just in case. Of course, since I only have a regular schoolbook-bag backpack, mine were simply attached via a bungee cord around the pack. I'm not much of a "gear nerd" in any area of life, and hiking is no different. The bungee cord system may not be ideal, but it works.

Soon we got to Crow's Clearing and went to the left side of the lot to the Big Crow trail, marked by a trail sign reading "Big Crow, 0.7 miles, Little Crow, 1.2 miles." There's also a trail for Hurricane Mountain on the right side of the lot, but that wasn't what we planned to do today.

We signed in at the trailhead register just past the Big Crow sign, and our Lake Placid 9'er winter challenge was officially underway.

The trail up Big Crow is short mileage-wise, but don't let that fool you—it packs a punch to the old legs and lungs. The beginning of the trail is a flat stroll through the woods, crossing a couple of streams that were partially frozen, but still had open water flowing through. But once the climb begins, it maintains a steep incline every step to the summit.

In the summer and fall, this mountain can be ascended very quickly because a large portion of the climb is on rock slabs that hikers can run up when it's dry. But on this day, thanks to some icy slabs, it wasn't quite as fast. Microspikes were all we needed, and the ice slabs didn't slow us down too dramatically, but it definitely was slower than normal.

Josh and I continued up the steep trail, digging our spikes into the ice hard with each step so we didn't slip and take a fall. Trekking poles helped tremendously as we went up the slabs. In fact, they were paramount going up and down. About halfway up, we came to the trail split for the Nun-da-ga-o Ridge to the right and Big Crow to the left. We went left and continued climbing. By this point, both Josh and I were sweating pretty heavily, which is something you want to avoid as much as possible during winter hiking. Sweat freezes, and that's not good for anyone in the mountains in the dead of winter.

We both took off our winter hats, which is a great quick way to cool off, and we unzipped our mid-layers to let some heat out and cool down. Worked like a charm. Though ultimately, I should have kept the mid-layer jacket in my backpack and hiked in just my base-layer shirt from the start. I was not "bold" and I did not start "cold." I started the hike off warm and comfortable. Lesson learned. Smaller mountains like the LP9 peaks are a much better place to learn these lessons than the bigger High Peaks.

It was still dark out with no sign of the sun yet, and we made our way up the final ice-covered slabs to the large, open rocky summit, standing at 2,815 feet for winter LP9'er number one of nine.

The summit has several cairns that lead you up and over the summit to Little Crow Trail if you're planning to do the Crow's loop, but that wasn't on our agenda today. Upon getting to the summit, we dropped our packs and enjoyed the silhouettes of the surrounding mountains, including twenty-eight different High Peaks. Big Crow certainly offers some stellar views for a very minimal effort.

It only took us around 25 minutes to summit Big Crow, including the extra walk from our van. The first time I hiked this peak in the summer, it took me 14 minutes from trailhead to summit. So it's small. Small but steep. And it's quite fun.

At this point, I walked to the far side of the summit, away from Josh, and I started recording some summit audio for my podcast, *The 46 of 46 Podcast*. Nothing quite tells the story of hiking in the Adirondacks than actually hearing the sounds of the Adirondack summits, right?

After roughly 30 minutes, the sunrise started to take shape, and what a view it was. And at this moment, Josh and I decided that a Christmas Eve sunrise hike would

An icy trail on Big Crow.

be our new tradition. The sun was shining and daytime had arrived, so we took off our coats, put them in our packs, and started back down the mountain.

It was at this point I was glad I didn't bring Wilson, my 105-pound silver labrador, today, because a few of these slabs were exceptionally challenging to get down thanks to the ice. In a few spots we had to really dig our spikes in and pray that they held with each step. One section of trail was probably a good 30 feet of ice-skating rink–caliber ice, a frozen river that would have been extremely dangerous to descend without traction like microspikes or snowshoes. I even snapped a photo of it because it was such a long stretch of pure, shiny ice. I'm positive Wilson would have struggled on some of these sections, so it's a good thing we left him home this morning.

But we eventually made it off the mountain safe and sound. We got back to Crow's Clearing and headed down the road back to the van. Still no sign of people yet, which means we had the entire mountain to ourselves.

We threw our gear into my van and drove down Hurricane Road to our next destination: the Baxter Mountain Trailhead off Route 9.

Baxter Mountain

We made it over to Baxter and began hiking up the quick and moderate 1.4-mile trail to the summit. Part of the Baxter Mountain Trail is on private property, and the landowner allows hikers to access the mountain on the trail. So it's even more crucial to respect the trail. You should treat every trail that way, but go above and beyond to be respectful on this one in particular.

Despite being only a couple of miles from Big Crow, this mountain was a drastically different scene. There was little to no snow anywhere on the mountain today. The trail was dirt covered with leaves, similar to a late fall hike. We left the snowshoes in the van for this one, and attached the microspikes to our packs and jingled our way up the mountain. Who needs jingle bells when you have jingle spikes? It was Christmas Eve after all.

The Baxter Trail is a great starter hike for someone who wants an easy, mellow hike up a mountain with outstanding views. It's excellent in every way—a gradual route with gentle climbs, switchbacks, and a well-groomed and marked trail.

Shortly after walking through a field with power lines, you're in the woods beginning the climb up. The woods were wide open since the trees were without their leaves this time of year. The switchbacks throughout this hike help make it easier on the old lungs and heart rate, unlike most Adirondack trails—especially in the High Peaks—that simply go straight up the mountain.

Up the dirt- and leaf-covered trail we went. Hopping from rock to rock at times, we soon came to a section that does require a bit of climbing. You climb up a couple of small boulders by grabbing onto some roots and pulling yourself up. But other than that short section, it's a pretty easygoing hike. After this climb we came out onto the first open ledge, a false summit of sorts. It often gets people thinking it's the true summit because of the great views. Josh went over to look, and I reminded him that this isn't the summit but we're almost there. We continued up the trail. From this point though, it's a quick trip to the true summit, which is marked by a cairn in the middle of some trees and brush, with views all around off the ledges.

Once at the cairn in the trees, the 2,440-foot Baxter Mountain was complete for winter Lake Placid 9'er number two of nine. The summit has a few different lookouts to enjoy the massive views Baxter has to offer, including a bunch of very recognizable pine trees you'll often see in hikers' summit photos. They have a Disney movie quality about them. When you see them, I guarantee you'll think, "Hmmm, those are some cool trees" and likely take a photo with them in the foreground and the mountains behind.

Like Big Crow, the Baxter summit overlooks tons of High Peaks as well as the LP9'er peak Hurricane Mountain. And if you look closely, you can see the Hurricane fire tower, very small on top.

While we were on the summit, I handed Josh his official Lake Placid 9'er patch, which I'd been meaning to give to him when he originally finished the LP9. Then we took in the overcast views for a while before beginning our descent down the mountain.

We moved quickly thanks to the partially frozen dirt ground that made for fast hiking conditions. Unlike Big Crow, there was no ice or snow to deal with on this peak today, so down the mountain we went, passing by the abundance of blowdown and pine trees all around as our feet crunched the season's leaves along the trail.

We made it off the mountain and back to the van in no time. Our Baxter trip was an hour and a half car to car, which included a long stay on the summit. I've hiked up this mountain in 19 minutes in the past, so it lends itself well to being a shorter hike worth staying on the summit for a long time to enjoy the amazing views.

I can't recommend this mountain enough. I knew most of my winter hikes would be much more winter-like than this one, but it was still a great hike as always. Now it was time to get back home and enjoy my other Christmas Eve traditions, one of those being what I call "Merry Squatmas," a heavy squat workout in my cold wooden shed known as Shedside Barbell.

So the squat rack was calling my name later today. Then tonight after church begins the Chinese food feast and the beginning of 24 hours of *A Christmas Story* on television. Our Christmas traditions were underway—let the festivities begin!

A Cobble Hill Christmas

Cobble Hill

Christmas morning arrived. Santa Claus came, and so did the sunshine. Gifts were given, smiles were had, and food was eaten. It was a great Christmas morning with the family. After our morning brunch with family, and with a flawless sunny day outside, Josh and I decided to get off the couch and go burn off some of those extra holiday calories.

A spontaneous Christmas hike up Cobble Hill on this bluebird Adirondack day was underway. My dog, Wilson the Silver Lab, and our friend Tom joined us. After

Christmas Day on Cobble Hill. TOM CRITELLI

suiting up and grabbing our gear, we drove uptown to the Cobble Hill trailhead parking just off Main Street Lake Placid (this was before the 2024 trailhead change), where a couple of cars were already parked. Likely some fellow Christmas hikers with the same idea. Can't pass up this perfect weather.

The trail up Cobble Hill starts with a wooden boardwalk through the woods. There was enough snow on the ground to cover the trail, so it was crunchy, but no snowshoes needed, just microspikes. We brought our snowshoes just in case, since we didn't know what the top would be like. My snowshoes were again bungeed to my pack. Not ideal, but it works.

Shortly into the hike, we came to the trail split for the 0.8-mile short trail and the 1.6-mile-long trail. The short trail is a steeper incline with some slab sections that are very much like hiking in the High Peaks. The longer trail along Echo Pond is a gradual switchback trail.

Today we opted to go up the short trail and down the longer trail to make a loop (note that the Long Trail is now closed as of the writing of this book). So we went straight and began climbing. The snow had filled in a lot of the trail, but the rocks were still poking out.

We moved up the trail hopping from rock to rock. After climbing over some blowdown and up a section, we rounded the bend to the left and came to the beginning of the rock slab—the cobble. You can actually see the rock slab when you're coming down the hill toward Main Street, as Cobble Hill sits in front of you across Mirror Lake.

This climb is a fun section of trail that even includes a rope tied to a tree as a makeshift railing to hold onto while you're climbing. It offers a unique vibe. This section of trail was a bit challenging for Wilson the Silver Lab, however.

Wilson took his own route up the slab, as dogs often do, but he eventually got to a point of no return—and he was stuck. The whimpering began and we had to go get him. We helped him down from the ledge that he was scared to move on, a bit frozen with fear. But he pulled it together quickly and hopped down. Classic Wilson.

We found a better route up for our canine companion, and he didn't have any more trouble climbing the trail. After climbing to the top of the slab, we headed back into the woods for the final short push to the summit, though not, of course, before we turned around on the slab to enjoy the big views of the village of Lake Placid and the other Adirondack Mountains. It's a terrific viewpoint.

Still no signs of other Christmas hikers yet despite seeing multiple cars at the trailhead. We continued up the trail, passing the final trail junction for the Long Trail, and about 100 feet later we came out of the trees onto the open rock summit. We were standing at 2,343 feet for winter Lake Placid 9'er number three of nine.

Cobble Hill, seen from all around Lake Placid, offers spectacular views of the High Peaks, like Marcy, Algonquin, Iroquois and the Boys, the slides on Colden, and Whiteface, to name a few. The summit also has views of LP9'er peaks Pitchoff and Van Hoevenberg, but the main stars of the summit scenery are the Sentinel Range above and the town of Lake Placid below.

It's truly an incredible experience to walk or drive on Main Street Lake Placid one minute and then just footsteps away start a quick hike up a little trail in the woods leading you to huge High Peaks views. I love Cobble Hill.

Once you reach the first section of the summit, make sure you walk across the summit to the other side where you'll see another trail going back into the woods. That takes you to a different area and viewpoint on the summit that has arguably even better views. I highly recommend going there.

I was layered up appropriately today, and the weather and temperature were quite comfortable. It was an amazing Christmas Day hike up Cobble Hill, now another Christmas Day tradition that we plan to continue next year.

We hung out up top for a good half hour, taking it all in on this Christmas afternoon. But it was Christmas after all, and time to get back to the family. So we started making our way back down, splitting off to go down the Long Trail this time to complete the loop. We made great time walking down the switchbacks, crunching our way one step at a time. Still no need for snowshoes but a definite need for microspikes.

Once off the mountain, the now-closed Long Trail runs along Echo Pond, a great quiet spot to take in some views at this hidden Adirondack pond before meeting up with the original trail taking us back to the car.

We encountered exactly zero people today, and once we got back to the trailhead, the other cars were gone. So we must have just missed each other on the trail. The winter hiking learning process continued, as I dialed in my layering more along with finding the right winter hiking pace to avoid sweating. A win for sure.

It turned out to be an excellent couple of hours here on this bluebird Christmas Day on our spontaneous hike up Cobble Hill, one of my favorite places in Lake Placid. Not many towns in the world can a person be walking on Main Street and a few minutes later be hiking up a mountain. This "hill" packs a punch and never gets old.

A Spontaneous Afternoon on Jo and Van Hoevenberg

Mount Jo

December 27, 2018. After a few days of recovering and coming out of my Christmas food coma, I decided what better way to burn off some calories than grab the boots and hit the trail.

It was around noon on Thursday when I thought, *I'd love to go for a hike today.* And since the LP9 mountains are all half-day or less hikes, they're the perfect option when you want to get into the woods spontaneously and enjoy a quick hike.

So I woke up Wilson the Silver Lab from one of his many afternoon naps, grabbed my backpack, got in the car, and drove over to the Adirondack Loj to hike local favorite Mount Jo. It's arguably the biggest bang for your buck in the Adirondacks in terms of difficulty-to-views ratio.

The way Mount Jo sits in front of the McIntyre Range is unbeatable, as Algonquin towers above, making for an iconic summit view. Especially on a mountain that only takes less than an hour to hike up.

Down the Adirondack Loj Road we went. Wilson and I soon arrived at the Adirondack Loj, where I paid my parking fee and found an available spot in the middle parking lot.

I made a game-time decision to leave the snowshoes in the car. I had a feeling based on the lack of snow we'd had lately along with the foot traffic Mount Jo gets that we wouldn't need the snowshoes—I was right.

I put the microspikes on my boots and we started walking toward the Mount Jo trail past the info/ticket booth.

The trail goes a few hundred yards through the woods before coming out to a trail along Heart Lake and a little cabin museum. Shortly after passing the museum, we came to the Mount Jo trail split on the right, and away we went.

The plan for today on this quick 2.6-mile hike was to take the short but steep trail up and the Long Trail down, making for a nice loop. The Short Trail weighs in at 1.2 miles one-way and is quite steep with High Peaks–caliber climbs, whereas the Long Trail offers a significantly gentler and more gradual climb, despite being slightly longer, and is more suitable for new hikers. Either way you choose, it's a great little hike that leads to huge Adirondack Mountain views.

We quickly came to the sign-in register where I signed us both in. Even on these small and easy trails, always sign in as it helps the DEC know how many people are using the trails, as well as being a potential lifesaver in an emergency (especially in the winter).

Right from the start, the trail winds its way up through the woods, gently climbing. The trail is a mix of small boulders and packed dirt, and thanks to the perfect amount of snow on the ground, the snow filled in a lot of the gaps between the rocks, making for a pleasing snow-covered sidewalk-like trail. Winter hiking is fast when the trails are like this. Wilson especially enjoyed it.

After 0.25 mile you reach the junction for the Short Trail and the Long Trail, marked by a wooden sign. The Long Trail continues straight, and the Short Trail goes right. Up the Short Trail we went.

I wasn't sure how Wilson would move today, but he was flying up the trail. I had to move fast to keep pace with him. We were cruising, to say the least. The Short Trail has some long and steep climbs, like what you'll find on most High Peaks. Steeply climbing up rock after rock for a good portion of the trail, you're constantly looking up to see if you're done yet. It can be a real gasser—one of those trails that gently reminds you that you still have a heart and lungs and quad muscles. Wilson jumped from rock to rock as if the snow and ice and boulders were meaningless to him, Meanwhile, I'm huffing and puffing behind, going as fast as I can to keep pace with this seven-year-old 105-pound silver lab.

One unique element of Mount Jo are the wooden signs throughout the Short Trail going from 1 to 10, with 10 being near the top. As you're climbing the numbers ascend, so you get a good feel for how far you are from the summit. It's roughly a mile up, so you can do the math as to when they appear.

Around halfway up, there's a big rock wall you'll walk along, and at this point I remember having to stop Wilson for a moment so I could get a few deep breaths in. Since I was sweating a little bit, something you don't want to do in the winter, I took off my hat and gloves. I put my gloves in my pack and my hat in my pocket—big mistake.

As we were climbing, passing groups on their way down, I realized it was colder than I thought, so I decided to put my hat back on, only to realize I had lost it.

At some point my hat must have worked its way out of my right pants pocket and fallen onto the trail. Great. I had this realization while chatting with a group on their way down. They watched me realize my hat was gone in real time.

"I seem to have lost my hat. If you happen to see a green Carhartt hat on the way down, would you mind grabbing it and putting it at the trail register for me?"

"Of course," the nice man responded. So off we went. Would I be reunited with my favorite hat? Only time would tell.

I was thoroughly impressed with Wilson's performance today on this crunchy, somewhat snow-covered, somewhat icy little mountain. Most of the rocks were bare on the way up, so my decision to leave the snowshoes in the car proved to be right. Microspikes were all I needed, but boy, were they definitely needed.

Once landing above the major climbs, after little wooden sign number 7, with around 0.2 mile or so to the summit, the trail levels off as the Long Trail and Short Trail meet before the final push toward the summit.

This stretch has several wooden planks to walk on, which of course were completely covered by snow on this late December day. Wilson behaved very well, stayed right next to me all day as he is wont to do. Soon we walked around the corner to the steep, snow-covered wooden staircase up the final boulders to the summit.

These stairs are actually new in the past few years and they're a major help. It's interesting looking back because I remember this section of Mount Jo being so challenging going up and down. And on a mountain typically used by new hikers and non-hikers alike, it's surprising that those stairs haven't been there forever.

Wilson took off up the stairs first, albeit slowly and cautiously. He was a bit nervous and awkward climbing them, but we made it up the slab, walked through the bushes, and arrived. Greeted by the enormous Mount Jo views of Algonquin, Iroquois, Wright, Boundary, Marcy, Colden, Street, Nye, and so many more High Peaks on top of this magnificent rocky summit. There we were standing 2,876 feet in the Adirondack sky for Lake Placid winter 9'er number four of nine.

The sky was overcast and the colors of the snow-covered peaks popped. The views were as good as anything we could ask for. There was one other person on the summit with us. We chatted briefly, and he mentioned he'd been up there for a few hours. Mount Jo is that type of mountain.

He was taking time-lapse photos, and with the moving clouds, I imagine those photos were probably incredible. It was 1:40 p.m. and officially had taken Wilson and I 25 minutes from trailhead to summit.

Just 90 minutes ago, I was at home with no intentions of hiking today, and then the thought hit my head. Now here I was, standing on a mountain summit taking in the always amazing Mount Jo views. A true perk to Adirondack living. Wilson and I stood there, looking around, enjoying the mountain views. The cold breeze started to blow though, and then it hit me—I really wish I had my hat right about now.

Since it was still early and Wilson had handled Mount Jo so well, I decided to head down and try to squeeze in a quick hike up one of my favorite Adirondack peaks, LP9'er Mount Van Hoevenberg. So we started back down the trail, down the wooden stairs, and across the flat snowy trail in the woods to the trail junction for the Long Trail.

The Long Trail was much icier than anticipated. This trail is a more gradual hike up and down with some cool rock walls along the route and easier on the heart, legs, and lungs. Many of the rock walls along the trail were covered in a 12-inch-thick blanket of ice from top to bottom. A fun visual during the winter season.

We passed several groups heading up Jo on this trail. Everyone was geared up well for the winter adventure, something you don't always see on this mountain.

Mount Jo and Heart Lake as seen from Wright Peak.

It's not too terrible on the legs and lungs, but it is a climb. The trail was obvious and broken out, and is well marked with trail markers.

It's important to note while winter hiking that just because there's a broken-out trail doesn't necessarily mean it's the actual trail. One hiker breaking out the trail could have been wrong and then everyone behind follows blindly thinking it's the correct path. This is not always the case, however (stay tuned for my hike up Bear Den). So it's important to be vigilant and focused, because you can never fully trust the trail from hikers ahead of you in the winter. Be mindful and do not blindly follow the tracks.

Wilson was climbing well, his energy remaining high. We continued ascending the mountain as I looked around at the open forest filled with naked, leafless hardwood trees and open views only visible in the winter months. LP9'er Pitchoff Mountain and the High Peak Cascade in particular peeked through the trees.

We continued up a few steeper, rugged sections (still no need for snowshoes). And after climbing one of these sections, I reached into my pocket to grab some of those delicious morsels known as peanut butter M&Ms.

My pocket was empty. Hmmm. I must have put them in my left pocket. So I took off my other glove and confidently reached into my left side pocket ready for a quick pick-me-up. Empty as well. So I reached back into my right pocket. I must have just not felt it. Nope. They're gone. At some point up the mountain, just like my winter hat less than a couple hours earlier on Mount Jo, my full, unopened bag of delectable peanut butter M&Ms had fallen out of my pocket.

I'd like to take this time to formally apologize to the always excellent Mount Van Hoevenberg, and the Adirondack Park as a whole, for the negligence I demonstrated on this day by littering an entire bag of chocolatey peanut buttery candy onto your majestic trails. It is with great sadness and self-disgust that I do not have that candy anymore and that I left a major trace where a trace shouldn't have been left. I will now take this time off to spend more time with my family as I reflect on my actions today. Cordially, James.

So yes. I accidentally lost the entire bag of M&Ms out of my pocket. I figured since the bag was bright and red that I would come across them on the way down, or that other hikers coming down would find them and pick them up, but only time would tell once again.

Wilson the Silver Lab and I carried on climbing, walking along a frozen drainage, climbing up some rocks, and stepping over blowdowns. The trail was coming back to me as we hiked.

After passing between two cliffs, the trail swings right, and it may seem like suddenly you're going the opposite way from where you thought you were going, but it's not. Just carry on. This portion of the trail dips up and down a good bit, making its way up the mountain's western ridge.

After dipping down, I saw another hiker up in front, the first one we had encountered on this trail. So we followed behind and soon caught up to her, and I noticed the abundance of patches on her backpack. Lots of hiking patches including a 46'er patch, Saranac Lake 6'er, and for the first time ever on trail, I saw an LP9'er patch. Having created the challenge earlier in the year, I was thrilled to speak with her.

Eventually, Wilson and I passed her as we made the final push to the summit, passing one more group, a mother, son, and their dog, as we hiked through some narrow stretches under the trees before coming out onto the summit ledge. What an exciting summit moment it is on Van Hoevenberg. There it was—my favorite view in the Adirondack Park.

The first ledge is not the true summit, so we went across the ledge back into the woods and hiked the remaining 50 yards or so up to the true summit, another set of ledges. Wilson and I took in the enormous, flawless mountain views; we were 2,940 feet up in the Adirondack Mountains sky for winter LP9'er number five of nine.

This summit has multiple large rock ledges with 180-plus-degree views. The mountain faces High Peaks like Algonquin, Iroquois, Wright, Colden, Marcy, and others, as well as Mount Jo. What makes this view special, however, is having South Meadows in front of those peaks. And the foliage view every fall is out of this world. Sweeping declaration: There's no better place for foliage views. The best views in the fall in the Adirondacks are on top of Mount Van Hoevenberg.

The ascent took us exactly 1 hour car to summit. Since it was just after 3:30 p.m., the sun was beginning to set. And since the days are just so darn short in the winter, we took in a partial sunset.

As we watched the golden sunset light up the sky and the snow-covered mountains around us, the hiker I passed earlier with the Lake Placid 9'er patch made her way to the summit. She was also working on the winter LP9. She had her camera and took a couple nice photos of Wilson and me together on the summit.

Despite the beautiful setting sun, it was time to get moving. I wasn't interested in hiking out in the dark today since I had Wilson with me. So down the trail we went like a couple of racehorses out of the gate. We were cruising. Hiking as fast as possible in an attempt to beat the sunset.

Off the summit ledges, through the woods. Up and down the dips in the trail, slipping and sliding, but moving forward at a great pace. Retracing our steps to reach the final stretch of the descent just before the beaver pond, where I paused to look for the lost bag of M&Ms. They were nowhere to be found. Bummer.

I figured a bright red bag of candy would be easy to spot in the white snow, but they were gone. I'm thinking perhaps the group with the dog I passed coming down as I was going up may have picked it up. I will never know. Maybe a Sasquatch treated himself to a pre-dinner snack? Anything's possible.

Soon we were off the mountain and back at the pond, circling back the way we came. And in typical Wilson fashion, he, of course, went right into the water like it was the middle of the summer. "Come on Wilson, get out of there!" The dog just loves to swim, what can I say?

We made it back around the pond to begin the final straight, flat mile walk to the trailhead at South Meadow Road. We moved fast, but about halfway I noticed

Mount Jo as seen from Van Hoevenberg.

Wilson lagging behind and moving slowly. Clearly he was tired from the big day. "Come on Wilson, almost there!"

We eventually made it back to the trailhead, signed out, and walked back to the car, beating the sunset. No headlamps needed. Wilson hopped in the back and immediately fell asleep as I jumped in the driver's seat and drove home.

What a great, spontaneous winter day of Adirondack Mountains adventure. Earlier today I was home eating lunch with no intention of hiking; fast forward an hour and Wilson and I were approaching the summit of Mount Jo. Smaller mountains like the many peaks of the LP9 allow for spontaneous adventure, which is exactly what we got today.

It was another successful winter day in the woods where Wilson the Silver Lab and I summited Mounts Jo and Van Hoevenberg—two of my favorite Adirondack Mountains—for Lake Placid winter 9'er peaks numbers four and five. Small mountains, giant views.

A great afternoon indeed.

Ice, Boulders, and Close Calls on Pitchoff

Pitchoff Mountain

December 30, 2018. As I continued warming up for winter hiking on these smaller yet exciting Lake Placid 9'er peaks, the next one up was another Lake Placid local favorite, Pitchoff Mountain.

My hiking and training partner, Josh, decided to come with me today to take in the cold winter Adirondack air. I was still dialing in the correct layers for my body while winter hiking, and today I wore thermal base layers on top and bottom, rain pants, and gaiters (nothing else on top).

I was quite chilly as we prepped our gear on the side of Route 73 at the Pitchoff Trailhead, across the street from the Cascade Mountain Trailhead, as the cars whipped past us one after the other on this late December morning.

I found today's layering system to work well for me and a step in the right direction for my own needs—I was cold while standing around, but comfortable while moving. So with this in mind, we quickly gathered our gear, bungeed my snowshoes to my backpack like usual, clipped on our microspikes, and walked up the wooden stairs into the woods.

We also made a game time decision to bring Wilson the Silver Lab with us on the hike, his biggest mountain to date. A decision that would result in quite a scare for us, as you'll learn later.

We signed in around 10 a.m., which for hikers like Josh and I, who always start in the High Peaks around 4:30 a.m., was a welcome change. One of the things I love about the LP9 mountains is that they're all small enough to decide the day of to go hiking. They don't always require the same amount of prep or planning as hiking in the High Peaks does. We only decided that morning to hike Pitchoff via the West Trail since it was a relatively clear day.

Pitchoff stands at nearly 3,500 feet in elevation, and is the only mountain in the entire Sentinel Range with a trail. It's a 4.8-mile out-and-back hike from the Cascade/Pitchoff Trailhead, though it can also be done as a traverse beginning or ending at the Pitchoff East trailhead farther down Route 73, which is 5.9 miles. The mountain has some steep sections to climb but offers an amazing experience at Balanced Rocks, a great location to spend some time while you're hiking this classic Adirondack peak.

We started moving up the trail. This trail has a lot of changing terrain and climbs as well as frequent boulder lookouts throughout the trip, so there's plenty of places to stop for views while climbing, with excellent vistas of Cascade Mountain and the Cascade Lakes below.

The first mile or so includes some gentle climbing as you make your way up above Route 73, down to your right. About a mile in we came to the first real climb of the day, which required a lot of grabbing onto roots and digging our microspikes into the ice with each step. The ice was thick today where water runs off the trail.

Wilson, however, would usually take it upon himself to find his own way up or around these icy sections, sometimes after a moment of light whimpering.

With all the leaves off the trees, the views throughout the hike were great. You're above Route 73 overlooking Cascade on one side, and then through the trees on the other side you can see Algonquin and some other High Peaks in the distance—views that are hidden most of the year because of the leaves on the trees.

James having fun at Balanced Rocks. JOSH BLISS

day it was here in the Sentinel Range. Lake Placid winter 9'er number six of nine was in the books. On to the next one.

A Winter Hurricane on Hurricane

January 27, 2019. Hurricane Mountain. A major fan favorite in the Adirondack Park—even rated best mountain in New York by *Outside Magazine* in 2019. And they're not wrong. This is an incredible mountain, start to finish, that offers a little bit of everything and ends with an awesome Adirondack fire tower atop a massive open summit.

The Hurricane fire tower in the dead of winter.

Josh and I planned to hike this peak the night before, so in classic "4:30 crew" fashion, we got an early start. Though not as early as usual since we were only hiking this one peak as opposed to going out into the High Peaks. My alarm went off at 4 a.m., I picked Josh up at 5 a.m., and we drove from Lake Placid to the trailhead in between Keene and Elizabethtown on Route 9N where we planned to hike via the southern approach. The trailhead parking is along both sides of the road, and it's easy to miss if you're not looking. It's just up the road from the Baxter Mountain Trailhead.

We pulled up to the trailhead and parked the car, quickly prepped our gear, closed the van door, and started hiking toward the woods up and over the huge pile of snow lining the road. Into the woods we went. Adventure awaits.

Hurricane Mountain via the southern approach is roughly 7 miles round-trip with just over 2,000 feet of elevation gain. The mountain boasts almost every type of Adirondack terrain in one jam-packed hike. Huge High Peaks views on its enormous open rock summit with an Adirondack fire tower put it over the top as one of the best hikes in the entire Adirondack Park, a mountain worth visiting over and over again.

We clicked on our headlamps and signed into the trailhead around 5:30 a.m. We were first on the day for sure. Right from the start the trail begins climbing for the first half a mile. And since this newer trail (2014) is so popular and well traveled, the trail was like a snow-covered sidewalk. The well-packed, probably 24-inch-wide, smooth, perfect trail made for a very fast hike. One of the perks of good winter hiking is no rocks and roots to deal with. We had our snowshoes on our packs but didn't need them to start the day, though we figured we might need them toward the summit.

About a mile in we made it to the now frozen marshy beaver pond. The trail skirts around the right side via some wooden plank bridges buried in snow. The scenery was great at this point too, with the mountains in the background and the pond in the foreground.

We continued hiking through the open hardwood forest. The trail maintains a consistent gain throughout the hike, with some steeper moments, but the majority of the time it's nice and gradual. Josh and I made good time as we hiked at a strong but maintainable pace. It was an extremely windy day so we were extra cautious, since at any point the wind could easily blow down any one of the hundreds of trees all around us.

And then we came to a section at the turn of a switchback. Josh and I both came to a halt and looked around the forest at all the trees. The burst of wind was blowing the trees around like an inflatable tube dancer at a used car dealership—it was a wild sight. We immediately picked up our pace even more, and even started running up the trail at one point to clear this specific section of trees. You never know if a tree will come down, and we didn't want to find out.

Soon the wind died down and we came to a meadow that I remembered well from hiking this mountain back in the spring. It's a great spot not far from the first lookout ledge. Since this trail has some switchbacks, unlike most Adirondack trails, it helps make the climb more enjoyable for the heart and lungs—another reason this hike is the whole package and was rated the best in New York. We passed through the meadow and continued to climb the hard-packed, snowy, sidewalk-like mountain trail.

Around 3 miles in we came to the first big ledge, and once again, so did the wind. This ledge offers great views on a clear day, as well as views of the fire tower and the summit above in the distance. This ledge makes the summit look a lot farther away than it actually is. We were being pelted with snow and wind here, so we headed back into the tree line after just a few moments of taking in the view.

A few minutes later we decided it was a good time to gear up for the summit since we were still only wearing our base layers on top. So we dropped our packs and suited up. I put on an EMS mid-layer fleece, along with a down puffy jacket and a rain/wind shell on top. I also switched to a new, less sweaty pair of gloves. Okay, I was ready for the windy Hurricane Mountain summit.

Josh was ready to go too. Then right before we started hiking, he stopped to put on his face protection—a neck warmer and ski goggles. Man, I wished I had those too. I told Josh he didn't need them and to let me use them instead. He disagreed. So I put on my hood, zipped my coat all the way, and pulled the drawstring on my hood so you could barely even see my face. I was ready to face the 60-mile-per-hour winds that awaited us on top of that beautiful open rock summit.

We continued up the trail, ready for the elements that awaited us as we passed the junction with the Crow's Clearing trail. It was time to leave the tree line for the summit. We took a minute to mentally prepare. Time to head into the wind. And it was intense.

The wind whipped and roared so loud and heavy that we couldn't even communicate because we couldn't hear each other, and we also couldn't see more than a few feet in front of us either. A total whiteout situation with the wind whipping snow and ice everywhere.

Then suddenly an enormous gust of wind blew both Josh and I a good 3 feet to the side at the same exact time. We both weigh over 200 pounds, plus the weight of our fully loaded backpacks, so that gives you a good idea of the type of wind on the summit.

We carefully pushed forward as we scrambled up the summit toward the fire tower. The 60-mile-per-hour wind continued to whip ice into the side of my face, and visibility remained minimal.

Since I didn't have ski goggles today, I had to hike with my right eye closed because the wind was destroying the whole right side of my face. Lesson learned. I bought some goggles later that day. But despite the whiteout wind, we finally made it to the base of the fire tower.

I looked up at the tower as it hovered over us like a skyscraper, considering what it would take right now to climb to the top of the tower in this monster wind. And then we glanced at each other, and as if we were in each other's brains, in unison we both said, "Nope!"

So we touched the fire tower and immediately began the trip back over the summit to get inside the tree line again as fast as possible. It was a very quick 30-second summit stay on this day (for good reason) as we stood 3,678 feet up in the windy Adirondack sky for Lake Placid winter 9'er number seven of nine.

The wind continued to whip us around back and forth, left and right, and we methodically chose our steps as we backtracked across the exposed summit. Climbing up and over the ledges, going from ledge to ledge, up and over the rocks, over this way, over that way. Finally, we made it back inside the tree line.

"Wow! That was quite the adventure," I said to Josh as we started back down the trail away from the summit and the powerful, hurricane-like wind. A fitting name for this mountain.

In typical fashion we began booking it down the mountain, moving as fast as possible. Before we knew it, we had made it back to that first open ledge where we saw the fire tower in the distance earlier. We prepared ourselves again and quickly went onto the ledge, out into the windy Adirondack sky, as the wind whipped snow and ice at us. And it was whipping indeed. Quickly we went across and back into the protected tree line.

Shortly after this point, we passed our first group of the day: a couple of French-Canadian women. We chatted for a short moment and warned them of the heavy winds to come. We hiked on, past the meadow, down the winter sidewalk-like trail, past the beaver pond, and toward the trailhead.

Just as we approached the trailhead, we passed another group, a couple of locals who were overly excited for the wind up top. It was certainly a wild experience, to say the least. I had never experienced wind of this caliber before this hike. We made it back to the trailhead, signed out, and headed toward the car.

What. A. Hike. An exciting day on Hurricane, a mountain that lived up to its name today. I can't say enough good things about this peak, especially hiking it from this southern approach. The 60-mile-per-hour winds didn't stop us from reaching the summit, though it certainly made for a unique and memorable winter mountain experience.

Quit, Grit, and Perseverance on Bear Den and Catamount

Bear Den Mountain

March 9, 2019. Less than two weeks left of the "official" winter hiking season. Of course, the winter conditions in the Adirondacks extend far into May sometimes, but for hiking challenges, there's only a couple of weeks left.

In an effort to complete my Lake Placid winter 9'er, today's plan was to head to Wilmington to hike the secret gem next to Whiteface known as Bear Den Mountain and the often-confusing animal of a mountain known as Catamount. The weather was perfect—crystal clear blue skies with temperatures in the low 30s. An excellent day to hit the trail.

My plan on this two-mountain day was to start with the 3.4-mile trip up Bear Den early in the morning, then drive over to Catamount and complete the steeper nearly 4-mile journey up this rugged, sometimes confusing peak, a mountain that's sometimes more challenging than many High Peaks. It was a perfect day to finish the winter 9'er.

Like always, I got an early start, leaving my house at 4 a.m. and driving to Wilmington.

The trailhead for Bear Den is at the Whiteface Mountain Ski Resort. I drove over the bridge with the gate and turned right toward the Bear Den lot and trailhead. Sometimes the gate is closed, in which case you just have to park in a different lot and then walk over to the trailhead, which isn't too far.

Thankfully the gate was open, so I went over the bridge to the Bear Den parking lot, where the trailhead sign is in the corner to the left. It's hard to miss it. At this pre-5 a.m. hour at Whiteface, there was very little activity going on, and it was a peaceful start to my day, with tons of stars in the dark sky.

I was quite excited to hike today because I had recently purchased a brand-new hiking pack that I got on sale at EMS—an Osprey Kestrel 48-liter pack that fit me very well. Up until this point, I did all my hiking with a regular schoolbook-bag-type backpack, which had served me very well throughout my entire 46'er journey and much more.

But I wanted a pack with a better way to strap on the snowshoes than just bungee-ing them around the pack. That was the main reason. I will say, though, after hiking with a pack that fits my torso correctly, it's truly an amazing difference. And while a fancy backpack isn't necessary, it is pretty nice to have.

I changed up my layering system today and tried something different per my buddy Eli. I wore base layers, gaiters, and basketball shorts over them, as opposed to my rain pants. I wouldn't need the rain pants and the gaiters would keep my feet and lower legs dry. Well, until I fell down, of course, but we'll get to that. And then when I fell down again, but yeah, we'll get to that too. On top I wore my usual base-layer Techwick long-sleeve shirt and a hat and gloves. I will say, this collection of layers was definitely the best yet for me in terms of keeping the sweat at bay.

I closed my van door, grabbed my backpack, and headed out. I clicked my headlamp on and signed into Bear Den at 5 a.m. And up the trail I went. I began with just my microspikes, as the trail below was hard and very packed down.

Bear Den begins with a flat, wavy trail through the woods before climbing, and once it starts climbing, it has some switchbacks throughout. But when the serious climbing does begin, it really doesn't let up until the top. So despite being a smaller mountain, it certainly makes your legs and your lungs work for it—as it should.

I hiked up the dark trail, crunching my way between trees, winding through the woods, hearing nothing but my footsteps over the sound of the dead winter's night silence all around me. The forest was quiet this morning.

Around half a mile into the hike, I came to the trail junction for the mountain biking trails. At this point you want to go left for the hike up to Bear Den.

This is where the trail begins to climb as well, as you walk on the ridge with the Ausable River down below. There are many trail markers for the first half of the trail, but the second half could use a few more. Hikers will want to pay extra attention.

At this point in the trip, I noticed the snow on the trail getting heavier and heavier. I decided to put on my snowshoes. Excellent, snowshoes activated. Now we're really winter hiking, right?

I continued up the trail along the Ausable River flowing down in the valley below. Then the trail came to a split. And when I say "trail," I simply mean the previous hikers' tracks that I was following while also looking for trail markers on the trees. It was a real fork in the road where I didn't quite remember there being a trail split. Decision time . . .

In my mind I remembered the trail beginning to climb eventually, and I felt like I had been walking along this ridge for a while. So I went left, thinking that that must be the proper route. Of course, a trail marker or two would help, but that's not always the case in the mountains. In fact, when hiking in the High Peaks it's rarely the case.

Going left led up a very steep section, and after a few minutes of climbing up and holding trees, digging my snowshoes in so they wouldn't slip (even though they constantly slipped), I started to think, *I don't think this is the right way*.

But I carried on anyway, following the previous hikers' tracks, thinking that maybe the winter bushwhack would eventually come out to the real trail. Midway up another steep section, I stepped right out of my snowshoe. Great! I grabbed the shoe, and in as clumsy a manner as you could ever imagine, I tried putting it back on while holding on to a tree, trying not to slide back down this 15-foot steep incline that I was stuck in the middle of.

Man, I wish I was more flexible, I'm thinking to myself. After a minute or two of fumbling around, I finally got the snowshoe back on and I kept hiking up. The trail I was following leveled out a little bit as I was walking across the ridge, but the tracks eventually came to a halting stop. They just simply disappeared. They had either been covered with snow, the person turned around, or they just vanished into thin air like a UFO.

I decided to continue and push farther, hoping I'd eventually see a trail marker or the trail, or more footsteps. But then it happened again: I stepped out of my snowshoe.

Okay, once again here I am in mid-thigh-deep snow on the side of a hill that's obviously not the trail, trying to hold on and not slide down while also trying to put my snowshoe back on again. And once again, it was a struggle. It was at this point that I thought to myself, *Dude, you know what? I am done winter hiking. This sucks.* The mountains have a funny sense of humor, don't they?

I finally got the snowshoe back on and decided to turn around and head back to the trail junction with footsteps I saw earlier. At that point maybe I'd see if the other trail was the correct trail. Maybe. But also, I'm still quitting. I'm definitely quitting winter hiking.

To make matters worse, while backtracking down those steep sections that had been hard to climb up, I was falling down left and right. Nothing was going right. I find in the winter that I struggle to keep my weight forward out of fear of tripping forward and falling on my face. But ironically all that actually does is keep my weight back, and then I slip and fall backward instead, thus defeating the purpose of trying not to fall. Instead of falling forward, I fall backward—constantly.

So down I went. Over and over again. Probably three times during this quarter-mile stretch. Needless to say, this hike was not going well. I eventually arrived back at the footsteps junction where I went left earlier.

I said to myself, *Okay. I'll take a quick look up the trail. But I don't feel like getting lost in the winter here in the woods by myself. So I'm probably just going to go home today because I hate this. Winter hiking sucks. I'm sick of hiking solo too. I'm done.*

But the mountains showed me mercy at that moment. Like a light from the heavens in the distance, I saw a trail marker 30 yards away. Finally, some confirmation that now I'm going the correct way. I needed that. I decided to continue up the trail; my winter hiking career would live to see another day.

Shortly after this point, the trail was covered with untracked snow, and I would break trail from here to the summit. Thankfully I was able to eyeball a number of trail markers while I was breaking trail.

The thing about this peak, and other winter peaks, is when the leaves are off the trees and the forest is so open, it feels like anything could be the trail. So I followed my gut, and fortunately I was able to find trail marker after trail marker as I hiked up the snow-covered mountain trail. A picture-perfect winter landscape, might I add. It was almost a shame to damage the perfect views with my snowshoes and my tracks, but you know, it's hiking.

Step after step in the 12- to 15-inch-deep snow I went, leaving nice long tracks in the snow with my snowshoes. Just before the summit, after following many trail markers and guessing which way the trail was supposed to go—and usually being right, thankfully—I met another set of footprints. Clearly someone else's bushwhacked trail.

Possibly the trail I followed earlier. I'll never know. But after passing a small wooden sign on a tree with an arrow that says Bear Den, I went left and shortly after came out on the open summit ledge. The golden light of the sunrise lit up Whiteface Mountain down below. It was excellent. In this moment I laughed to myself about my hike up. The mountains will always test us, that's for sure. I'm glad I pressed on

A mid-hike winter sunrise through the empty trees on Bear Den Mountain.

to stand on the summit of Bear Den Mountain at 2,650 feet for Lake Placid winter 9'er number eight of nine.

The summit here has many different areas. It's actually a large summit, so you can explore while you're up there, but once you come out on a rocky ledge and see Whiteface majestically towering above, you're there.

I sent a photo of the view of Algonquin from Bear Den to a buddy of mine who was hiking Algonquin on the same day at the same time, and then he sent a photo back. It's always neat knowing that while you're standing on one of these mountains, there are other people currently climbing up the other mountains that you're looking at, having their own unique adventure.

It took me 1 hour and 35 minutes to summit today, which was significantly longer than in the summer, basically double the time. But between going the wrong way, backtracking, gear malfunctions, and breaking trail, it's not surprising. I stayed for a good 15 minutes and enjoyed the sun rising before I started back down the trail.

Earlier I mentioned my constant sliding and falling backward. On this descent, I decided to start leaning forward more and just commit to it. And I basically started skiing down the trail in my snowshoes. It was fast and actually very fun on this powdery snow trail.

I made incredible time down as I skied the trail, ducking and dodging trees like an Olympic downhill skier going through the flags and gates. Once I made it back to the footsteps trail junction from earlier, I laid some branches over the wrong trail to hopefully alert other hikers that this isn't the way to go.

Toward the bottom, I met my first other hikers of the day, and I told them about the correct trail, hoping they could avoid the confusion that I had experienced and stay on my freshly broken trail. There's another life lesson here. Just because there's tracks from previous people doesn't necessarily mean it's the correct way to go.

I made it off the mountain in about 35 minutes. When signing out, I saw that a few days earlier another guy named James had signed in attempting to do the LP9 Winter Ultra, which is all nine mountains in the winter in 24 hours. Wild. I later learned that he wasn't able to finish it that day due to cramping, but tried again a couple weeks later with another guy named Jacob, and they both finished, becoming the first Lake Placid 9 Winter Ultra finishers. So impressive.

I walked back to my van feeling proud that I kept going when my mind was quitting on me, ultimately saving the day, hike, winter LP9 journey, and even my "winter hiking career." Bear Den will always hold a funny place in my heart because of this hike.

Time to head to Catamount for my final Lake Placid winter 9'er peak.

Catamount Mountain

It's a good 10- or 15-minute drive to the Catamount Trailhead from Bear Den. There are few mountains that look as grand from the road as Catamount. As you drive down Plank Road, you eventually leave some trees and the mountain suddenly appears, towering above the road in the most majestic of ways. You'll know the second you see it: That's the mountain you're about to hike. It stands alone both geographically and metaphorically. Catamount is one of a kind, and a true hidden Adirondack gem.

I pulled into the trailhead parking lot and gathered my gear. Minutes later, another car with a group of four hikers pulled into the parking lot. We started chatting and I learned that all four of them were also finishing up their own winter LP9 challenge today on Catamount. So we had a lot in common, and as the creator of the challenge it was both exciting and humbling that they were tackling this journey. It was time to climb the rugged Catamount Mountain to finish my winter Lake Placid 9.

Catamount is one of the classic medium-sized Adirondack hikes, standing just under 3,200 feet elevation with 1,500 feet of elevation gain. The hike is roughly 4 miles round-trip and includes memorable scrambles, a notorious chimney climb, and an open summit with 360-degree views, all offering an unparalleled Adirondack hiking experience. A mountain worth visiting many times over.

I signed into the trail just after 8 a.m. and the day began. I had snowshoes strapped on my pack and microspikes on my boots. The first half mile or so is a flat walk in the woods as you approach the peak. Thanks to perfect winter conditions and minimal snowfall this week, the trail was already broken out, packed down, and fast, making the approach a breeze.

The hiking trail passes an ATV trail and runs along private property during this approach, but just stay to the right on the hiking trail. Soon I came to the base of the mountain and began ascending. The terrain is moderate to steep for almost the entire ascent, gaining a good 1,300 feet elevation in a mile, so you're really working hard for this summit.

Thankfully, the sidewalk-like trail made the hiking fast today. I weaved my way up the mountain between the empty birch trees toward Catamount's false summit, visible above for a large chunk of the ascent. The trail's consistent climb had my heart beating as I crunched my way up, one foot in front of the other. I found myself stopping every so often for a few seconds to enjoy a couple long, deep breaths before continuing the climb. The legs were burning today for sure—in a good way.

As I was breathing heavily, I reminded myself that nobody was forcing me to be out here huffing and puffing; I could be at home *not* huffing and puffing. I'm voluntarily choosing to do this. Why? Hiking—what a wild concept, right? These thoughts often run through my head during moments of heavy breathing on the trail. I typically remind myself that it's a privilege to have the ability and health necessary to hike up a mountain and do hard things. Perspective is key. The mountains certainly teach us a lot of lessons if we're willing to look for them.

I could often hear chatter in the distance from the hikers below me on the trail, which gave me motivation to keep pushing on so as not to be passed—some minor and meaningless motivation to keep on up the trail. Whatever works, I suppose.

The steady incline continued, and soon I arrived at the infamous "Catamount Chimney," located just below the false summit. The chimney is a steep, narrow cutout in the rock slab that only fits one person at a time, which you need to climb up to continue to the summit. It's arguably the most memorable 20-foot stretch of "trail" on the LP9.

If heights or any sort of climbing using your hands scare you, this portion may be a bit challenging. But overcoming challenges and conquering fears in life is what it's all about. So use this mountain as a source of growth. The chimney is pretty fun too, because it's unique, so keep that in mind. And once you finish climbing up onto the slab above it, the views are amazing.

Today I decided to film myself climbing the chimney to get a good first-person-perspective video to show my wife. I took my phone out of my backpack, turned on the camera, and wedged it against my chest and the pack's chest strap, with nothing holding it there other than the pressure. Then I started up the chimney.

Thanks to the conditions, the climbing was actually easier today than it is in the summer because of the added snowpack raising me higher up on the trail, which made it easier to hold on to the rocks while climbing. Keep in mind that if the rock is covered in ice, it's even more dangerous, and practically unclimbable sometimes without crampons. But today it was as perfect as it could be. So up I went, through the chimney like Santa Claus. My phone remained intact, filming what I hoped would be a great little video perspective of this memorable stretch of the trail.

I made it to the top without issue. Victory. I stood up and turned around to take in the views—but then it happened.

The phone slipped out of my chest strap—in what felt like slow motion—tumbled onto the ground, and flipped and flopped its way down the entire chimney to the bottom. Just as I had felt victorious on top of the chimney, the mountain chopped me down a peg or two. The mountains are good for that; they keep us humble.

Now I had to climb back down the chimney, grab my phone, and then climb back up a second time. Classic. Serves me right. So down I went, grabbed the phone, and climbed back up. I left my pack at the top, so it was a little quicker this time. Shortly after, I found myself on top of the false summit, with the true summit towering ahead. Sometimes people stop at the false summit since it's a huge open rock area with views as great as anywhere, but today I was heading to the top. I continued on the trail marked by cairns back into the woods.

This next stretch of trail had me in much thicker woods before coming out onto various slab scrambles. From here on, the trail gets a bit tricky to follow. There's one place in particular that could really use one or two more trail markers (I've missed a turn twice on this mountain). Just be vigilant looking for trail markers and signs of the correct path. You will be climbing up onto ledges, but you're never rock climbing. So if you're at a rock wall, it's not the correct path.

The last stretch of this hike is above the trees and has you following cairns, blazes on the rock, and trail markers, making a zigzag scramble to the top. I know many people have hellish winter days on this mountain, but that wasn't the case today thanks to the sunny, calm conditions.

I continued up the open slab toward the summit and then I was there, greeted by another hiker named Brant, whom I had coincidentally exchanged messages with online in the past.

A few steps later I arrived at the true summit, the wonderful, open summit with views to the end of the world, at 9:40 a.m., roughly 90 minutes after signing in. I took in the 360-degree summit views, staring at Whiteface, Esther, Moose, McKenzie, and so many more for Lake Placid winter 9'er number nine of nine.

Winter LP9 complete! Well, almost. I still had to get down the mountain, of course.

I was thrilled to have earned that blue Winter 9'er patch here during the first winter LP9 season. Brant and I chatted for a good 20 minutes before he started down the trail as I stayed up top. I wanted to give the group of hikers I met in the parking lot the Winter 9'er patch so they could have it for their summit photos.

I waited for another 15 minutes because I kept hearing their voices in the distance, and they sounded close. Sound truly does carry in the mountains—it sounded like they were just below the summit, but that wasn't the case.

Down the trail I went, backtracking my footprints, zigzagging off the rock summit, scrambling down, making sure I didn't pick up too much speed because a slip and fall could be disastrous. I took my time getting back into the tree line, and soon I was there.

I continued my newly learned technique of skiing down the trail on my feet, which helped make it fun and fast, with fewer falls (though still some falls). I eventually found the group of hikers from earlier in the day. They were much farther down the trail than I thought based on hearing their voices from the summit. It was strange yet impressive that I could hear them as clear as if next to me from the summit. Let this be a warning not to trash-talk other hikers on Catamount because they'll probably hear you on the mountain, resulting in an awkward moment on the trail when you pass each other. Nobody wants that, right?

We had a quick conversation and I handed them the patch. I told them to decide among themselves who keeps it. My simple gesture was met by an overwhelmingly enthusiastic response by all four of them. It even brought one woman to tears because of what this winter LP9 challenge meant to her and what she overcame throughout her journey. I'm willing to bet she is the one who kept the well-earned patch. The patch becomes a tangible representation of the memories, the adventures, and for some, the person they became on the journey. It's truly amazing to see how much these mountains mean to people and the transformation that mountains can inspire in people's lives. It isn't "just hiking" for many people, it's much more.

The five of us took a photo together, then went our separate ways. They climbed to the summit and I continued skiing down the mountain. Up and over the false summit I went, and soon I was back at the chimney to climb down it the second time today.

After the chimney, I passed a younger couple and their dog, who asked me about the chimney. Fortunately, after four times through it today, I had a good idea.

Later I reconnected with this couple on the Adirondack hiking Facebook group. In fact, I met eight people total on both mountains today, and I reconnected with six or seven of them within 24 hours thanks to seeing their photos in various ADK hiking Facebook groups. What a time to be alive.

I made excellent time descending the mountain, skiing down on my snowshoes, my speed worthy of an Olympic silver medal. Yes, silver, not quite gold yet.

Once I was off the trail, I caught back up with Brant, the hiker I met on the summit, and we walked out together to finish the day. Soon we arrived at the trailhead and I signed out.

Officially a Lake Placid Winter 9'er

I had another successful winter day in the woods and completed another successful Adirondack hiking challenge. Today's hikes of Bear Den and Catamount Mountains marked numbers eight and nine of nine on my Lake Placid winter 9'er journey. What an adventure it was.

My experience and confidence in winter hiking here on the ninth mountain compared with the first was dramatic. The LP9 once again proved to be a perfect list of mountains to prepare someone for hiking in the Adirondacks—in the summer and winter. Hiking smaller peaks that one by one get bigger and bigger, ultimately prepares people to confidently hike in the High Peaks. I highly recommend these mountains to anybody looking for a great Adirondack hiking experience.

You'd be hard-pressed to find a better and more diverse Adirondack hiking experience, and I encourage anybody to give these mountains a try. I had an awesome time learning and getting comfortable winter hiking, dialing in my layers and gear on these smaller mountains, without the added pressure of being deep in the Adirondack backcountry if things didn't go well. I can't say enough good things about all nine of these mountains.

Thank you for reading my journey through the winter LP9. I hope these mountains teach you as much about hiking, the outdoors, the world, and yourself as they taught me.

Enjoy the journey!

Whiteface Mountain seen from the summit of Catamount.

Other Hikes

Other Adirondack Hiking Challenges

Hiking challenges are part of the hiking culture in the Adirondacks. It's the Adirondack brand. Every list of mountains offers new experiences and fresh adventure, and brings hikers to new corners of the Adirondack Park. Once you finish the Lake Placid 9, there are many more challenges to tackle and mountains to explore, including the following:

Saranac Lake 6'er
These six mountains are located around the Saranac Lake region. They form a journey similar to the LP9 with some medium-sized mountains that will prepare hikers for the larger High Peaks. Peaks include:

- McKenzie Mountain—3,822 feet
- Ampersand Mountain—3,353 feet
- Scarface Mountain—3,054 feet
- Haystack Mountain—2,864 feet
- St. Regis Mountain—2,874 feet
- Baker Mountain—2,452 feet

Tupper Lake Triad
These three mountains are all around the Tupper Lake region, and all three make a fun day's hike, including a fire tower on Mount Arab. These are short mountains, perfect for the family or a quick afternoon hike. Peaks include:

- Mount Arab—2,545 feet
- Coney Mountain—2,280 feet
- Goodman Mountain—2,178 feet

Lake George 12'ster
These twelve peaks are all around the Lake George region and make a terrific ADK mountain adventure. Peaks include:

- Black Mountain—2,659 feet
- Buck Mountain—2,334 feet
- Five Mile Mountain—2,255 feet
- Erebus Mountain—2,526 feet
- Huckleberry Mountain—2,242 feet
- Sleeping Beauty Lookout—2,242 feet
- Cat Mountain—1,955 feet

- Thomas Mountain—1,904 feet
- Brown Mountain (Tongue Range)—1,987 feet
- Fifth Peak (Tongue Range)—1,814 feet
- French Point Mountain—1,756 feet
- First Peak (Tongue Range)—1,593 feet

Fulton Chain Trifecta

In the Old Forge region, this challenge is lovely because the three mountains are close together, feature shorter hikes, and offer great lake views and a fire tower. They are another great group of peaks that can be hiked in a single afternoon and are perfect for the family. Peaks include:

- Bald Mountain (Rondaxe Fire Tower)—2,350 feet
- Black Bear Mountain—2,454 feet
- Rocky Mountain—1,759 feet

Mountain Views Without Hiking for Them

While nothing approaches the fulfillment that comes from hiking up a mountain and earning that summit view, sometimes it's nice to enjoy the scenery with less effort. Plus, hiking is not for everyone, so this gives everyone a chance to enjoy the mountain views in some way. Below are some of my favorite places around the Lake Placid and High Peaks region to take in big Adirondack views right from your car.

I'm also willing to bet if you have a loved one who isn't sure if they want to try hiking, seeing these views may change their mind. Who knows, maybe they'll join you on your next hike.

Crown Plaza Resort—Lake Placid

One of the most amazing views of the Adirondack High Peaks is at the Crown Plaza Resort on Main Street Lake Placid. The view from the back parking lot is as good as it gets. The resort is on top of a hill overlooking the village and gives a perspective that is unmatched anywhere else. You don't even have to get out of your vehicle. I've parked here many times and enjoyed a quick lunch with a view from my driver's seat. It's also a great place to stay when you're visiting Lake Placid.

Route 73 and Adirondack Loj Road Intersection

This view is the quintessential Adirondack High Peaks view, the type of view that postcards are made of. You'll see the mighty MacIntyre Range, Colden, Marcy, Street, Nye, Mount Jo, and many other mountains. There is a pull-off immediately upon turning onto Adirondack Loj Road. You'll want to take some pictures here, I guarantee it.

The Route 9N Hill

Driving west on Route 9N down the hill toward Route 73 will give you one of the biggest views in the park, right from your car. You'll come around a turn and be hit with an unparalleled view of the Sentinel Range that will feel otherworldly. Fortunately for LP9 hikers, the Baxter Mountain trailhead is at the top of this hill (Route 9N). If you drive back toward Keene/Lake Placid after hiking Baxter (or Hurricane just up the road), you'll automatically drive down this hill. You'll know the view once you see it because you'll simply say, "*Wow!*"

Whiteface Mountain Memorial Highway, aka "the Toll Road"

The Whiteface Mountain Memorial Highway runs up Whiteface Mountain. It's the only mountain with a road to the summit. The toll road is open daily from 8:45 a.m. to 5:30 p.m. from late May through Columbus Day weekend in October. Enjoy a High Peak summit view without the effort of hiking it. I highly recommend this drive during the fall foliage season.

I-87 to Lake Placid

The drive from I-87 through Keene Valley all the way to Lake Placid is unmatched. You'll likely drive this road on your way to Lake Placid, and it never gets old as you travel through the mountains, along the edge of mountains through the Cascade lakes. I've driven it hundreds and hundreds of times and am in awe every time.

The Wilmington Notch

The drive from Lake Placid to Wilmington/Whiteface/Bear Den/Catamount on Route 86 will have everyone staring out the window in wonder. Like the drive from I-87 to Lake Placid, the "Wilmington Notch" travels through the mountains and along the mighty Ausable River in the most pleasing of ways. During peak foliage this road is worth many trips through it.

Time to Hit the Trail

Final Words

The Lake Placid 9'er is more than just a list of nine mountains. For some, it's the start of a hiking journey that leads deeper into the Adirondacks and beyond. For others, it's a chance to explore new mountains in a new area. These mountains have launched thousands of adventures, and now it's your turn.

Baxter Mountain trees as the sun begins to set.

As you finish this book, I want you to know this: You're ready for the mountains. You've got the knowledge and the tools to have a successful adventure, and it's time to take those first steps. Along the way you'll discover that the mountains aren't just about pretty views—they also show you what you're capable of. They teach you how to do the hard things and keep taking the next step toward the summit. If you ask me, that's the real gift the mountains give us.

My hope is that the LP9 continues to do what it was created for—to showcase the beauty of the smaller mountains around Lake Placid, and to give novice hikers a plan to take their first steps on a trail and build the confidence to hike farther. The outdoors has a way of changing us if we let it. May these trails always inspire you to keep going farther.

So grab your pack, lace up your boots, and hit the trail. Your Lake Placid 9'er adventure starts now!

LP9 Website

For more information about the LP9 or to submit your finisher's registration, visit our website at www.LakePlacid9er.com.

James taking in his favorite view in the ADK for the millionth time—never gets old.

Beyond the Trail

James on Rocky Peak Ridge while guiding a hike for his Great Range Athlete MARCY team.
PATRICK ROHR

Other Books by James Appleton

The Adirondack 46 in 18 Hikes: The Complete Guide to Hiking the High Peaks
Everything you need to know for a safe and successful 46'er journey, start to finish. This guide lays out a complete hiking itinerary alongside the transformative story of the author's first round of the Adirondack 46. Offering all the information of a guidebook, it reads like an adventure book.

Adirondack Campfire Stories: Tales and Folklore from Inside the Blue Line
A collection of campfire tales set in and around the Adirondack Park. Some are true, some are fiction—but they all capture the spirit of the ADK mountains. Spooky, fun, and full of Adirondack lore in familiar places, these stories will leave you looking over your shoulder on your next High Peaks hike.

Hike Strong: The Complete Guide to Building Strength, Endurance, and Confidence for Hiking and Backpacking
A complete training system built on James's own "Mountain-Strength Method," a training system that's helped hundreds of hikers worldwide improve their physical fitness for the trail. Learn how to strength train, what exercises translate directly to hiking, and how to fuel your body with smart nutrition—on and off the trail.

Available wherever you get your books.

Work with James

Hiking mountains isn't just about the summit views, the miles on the trail, or the elevation you gain—it's about building the strength, endurance, and confidence in yourself to do the hard things that lead to the summits of life. That's exactly what I help hikers do through my various coaching programs and guide services.

Seek to Do More: One-on-One Online Coaching Program
My one-on-one holistic coaching program has helped over one hundred people worldwide transform their physical fitness on the trail, and their nutrition, mindset, habits, and discipline off the trail. Together we'll build a strong body, resilient mind, and disciplined lifestyle that carries you farther than you ever thought possible.

For people who want to improve their ability in the mountains and transform how they show up in every area of their life.

Learn more at www.seektodomore.com.

Great Range Athlete: Team Training Program

My six-week online group training program is built specifically for hikers. This group coaching program has helped over 300 hikers around the world build strength, endurance, and confidence to enjoy stronger mountain adventures. You'll also gain a new community of like-minded hikers who will become like family in the process.

For both new and seasoned hikers looking to elevate their ability to have better mountain adventures.

Learn more at www.greatrangeathlete.com.

Hiking Guide Services

I'm a New York State licensed hiking guide offering guided hikes in the Adirondacks. Whether you're looking to hike your first mountain, tackling a challenge like the Lake Placid 9, or working toward the Adirondack 46, I'll make sure you're prepared and supported every step of the way.

Learn more at www.46outdoors.com.

Connect with James

www.46outdoors.com

james@46outdoors.com

@jamesappleton46

@46Outdoors

The 46 of 46 Podcast

www.46outdoors.com

THE TEN ESSENTIALS OF HIKING

American Hiking Society

American Hiking Society recommends you pack the "Ten Essentials" every time you head out for a hike. Whether you plan to be gone for a couple of hours or several months, make sure to pack these items. Become familiar with these items and know how to use them. Learn more at **AmericanHiking.org/hiking-resources**

1. Appropriate Footwear

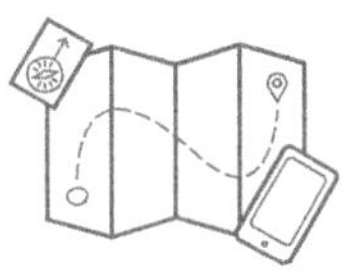

2. Navigation

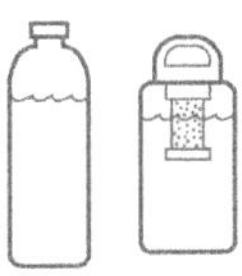

3. Water (and a way to purify it)

4. Food

5. Rain Gear & Dry-Fast Layers

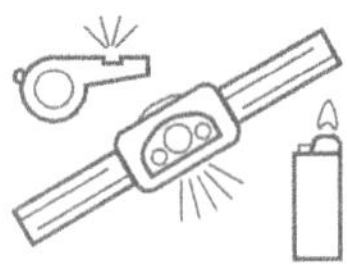

6. Safety Items (light, fire, and a whistle)

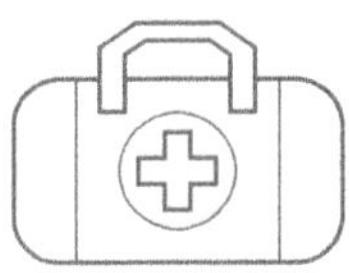

7. First Aid Kit

8. Knife or Multi-Tool

9. Sun Protection

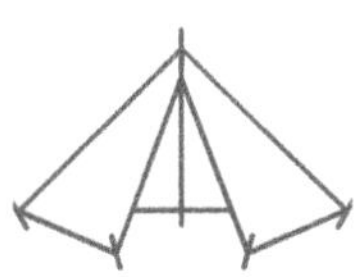

10. Shelter

www.ingramcontent.com/pod-product-compliance
Ingram Content Group UK Ltd.
Pitfield, Milton Keynes, MK11 3LW, UK
UKHW051823010926
8330IPUK00003B/27

9 781493 096008